Prayer Journal

S0-CFJ-413

OPENING
THE WORD

ADVENT TO PENTECOST

EDWARD SRI
General Editor

YEAR C
BOOK 1

Nihil obstat: Ben Akers, STL
Imprimatur: Most Rev. Samuel J. Aquila, Archbishop of Denver

Copyright © 2012 Augustine Institute. All rights reserved.
With the exception of short excerpts used in articles and critical reviews, no part of
this work may be reproduced, transmitted, or stored in any form whatsoever, printed or
electronic, without the prior permission of the publisher.

Excerpts from the Lectionary for Mass for Use in the Dioceses of the United States of
America, second typical edition © 2001, 1998, 1997, 1986, 1970 Confraternity of Christian
Doctrine, Inc., Washington, D.C. Used with permission. All rights reserved.
No portion of this text may be reproduced by any means without permission in writing
from the copyright owner.

Some Scripture verses contained herein are from the Catholic Edition of the Revised
Standard Version of the Bible, copyright ©1965, 1966 by the Division of Christian
Educators of the National Council of the Churches of Christ in the United States of
America. Used by permission. All rights reserved.

English translation of the Catechism of the Catholic Church for the United States of
America, copyright ©1994, United States Catholic Conference, Inc.—Libreria Editrice
Vaticana. English translation of the Catechism of the Catholic Church: Modification from
the Editio Typica copyright ©1997, United States Catholic Conference, Inc.—Libreria
Editrice Vaticana.

Presenters: Ben Akers, Jim Beckman, Tim Gray, Mary Healy, Julianna Miles, Scott
Powell, Father John Riley, Edward Sri

Contributing Writers: Ben Akers, Jim Beckman, Ashley Crane, Sean Innerst, Woodeene
Koenig-Bricker, Carmen Kamrath, Julianna Miles, Lucas Pollice, Scott Powell, Edward Sri,
Deacon Rev. Dennis Walters

Assistant Editor: Lucas Pollice

Media Production: Brenda Kraft, Justin Leddick, Kevin Mallory

Graphic Design: Stacy Innerst

Augustine Institute
6160 South Syracuse Way
Greenwood Village, CO 80111
Orders: 303-937-4420
OpeningtheWord.org
AugustineInstitute.org

Printed in the United States of America
Library of Congress Control Number: 2012908767
ISBN 978-0-9847868-1-7

TABLE OF CONTENTS

An Introduction to Opening the Word

Welcome to Opening the Word. Over the next several months, we are going to be exploring sacred Scripture, prayer, and insights about how the Lord is working in our midst today. We invite you to participate fully in this study, allowing the Father to guide you, the Son to extend his love to you, and the Holy Spirit to enlighten your heart and mind.

This Prayer Journal is your own personal journal for you to use as we open and explore the Sunday Readings. Using this journal for your individual reflection, journaling, and prayer will help you to understand the Sunday Readings and make them come alive in your daily life. It is an opportunity for you to truly encounter Christ in the Word of God and invite him more deeply into your heart.

Your journal contains the Readings for each particular Sunday for your personal reading and reflection and then leads you through a week-long study, reflection, and meditation on the Sunday Readings so that the Word of God can truly be active and applicable to your everyday life. For each Sunday, your Prayer Journal leads you through the traditional prayerful reading of Scripture known as Lectio Divina, which can be done in a group setting or on your own. Then there are personal reflection and meditation questions as well as an inspiring quote from sacred Scripture, the Catechism of the Catholic Church, a saint, or a spiritual writer for each day of the rest of the week to help the Scripture Readings come alive in your day-to-day life.

We have found that when our participants prayerfully use this journal with an open heart, they don't just grow in their understanding of sacred Scripture, but their relationship with our Lord also grows. Going to Mass on Sunday is never the same again, as they are able to hear the Sunday Readings in a much more personal way.

We're excited for you as you begin your journey into the Sunday Readings!

AN OVERVIEW OF LECTIO DIVINA

Lectio Divina is an ancient practice to enhance one's prayer life through the power of God's Word. The term itself means "divine reading" of the sacred Scriptures. It is our hope that by using these simple steps each day as you study the Scriptures of Opening the Word, you will develop an effective way to soak up God's Word as you learn to fruitfully pray and listen to how God wants to be part of your life.

Here is a brief description of each step of Lectio Divina for your reference as you engage Scripture through this practice:

Sacred Reading of the Scriptures *(Lectio)*: The reading and rereading of the Scripture, paying close attention to words, details, themes, and patterns that speak to the reader.

Meditation *(Meditatio)*: Meditating or reflecting on what's been read to gain understanding. Allow the Holy Spirit to guide you as you spend time pondering what you have read and striving to understand it in meditation.

Prayer *(Oratio)*: A time to bring our meditative thoughts to God in prayer. Talk with God about how the connections and implications of your meditation on the Scripture affect your life and the lives of those around you.

Contemplation *(Contemplatio)*: A time of quiet and rest, when we become the receiver and listen to God's voice. Contemplation is a gift from God, not something we achieve on our own—so be patient as you practice this step and strive to be receptive to God's voice speaking into your life.

Resolution *(Operatio)*: A call for resolution and action, inviting us to respond to the things we have read in Scripture and have prayed about and to put them into practice.

(To learn more about Lectio Divina, check out Dr. Tim Gray's book **Praying Scripture for a Change**, available at www.AscensionPress.com.)

1ST SUNDAY OF ADVENT
YEAR C

A NEW BEGINNING

READINGS FOR THE
FIRST SUNDAY OF ADVENT

FIRST READING
- Jeremiah 33:14-16 -

The days are coming, says the Lord, / when I will fulfill the promise / I made to the house of Israel and Judah. / In those days, in that time, / I will raise up for David a just shoot; / he shall do what is right and just in the land. / In those days Judah shall be safe / and Jerusalem shall dwell secure; / this is what they call her: / "The Lord our justice."

RESPONSORIAL PSALM
- Psalm 25:4-5, 8-9, 10, 14 -

R: **To you, O Lord, I lift my soul.**

Your ways, O Lord, make known to me;
teach me your paths,
guide me in your truth and teach me,
for you are God my savior,
and for you I wait all the day.
R:

Good and upright is the Lord;
thus he shows sinners the way.
He guides the humble to justice,
and teaches the humble his way.
R:

All the paths of the Lord are kindness and constancy
toward those who keep his covenant and his decrees.
The friendship of the Lord is with those who fear him,
and his covenant, for their instruction.
R:

SECOND READING

- 1 Thessalonians 3:12-4:2 -

Brothers and sisters: May the Lord make you increase and abound in love for one another and for all, just as we have for you, so as to strengthen your hearts, to be blameless in holiness before our God and Father at the coming of our Lord Jesus with all his holy ones. Amen. Finally, brothers and sisters, we earnestly ask and exhort you in the Lord Jesus that, as you received from us how you should conduct yourselves to please God—and as you are conducting yourselves—you do so even more. For you know what instructions we gave you through the Lord Jesus.

GOSPEL

-Luke 21:25-28, 34-36 -

Jesus said to his disciples: "There will be signs in the sun, the moon, and the stars, and on earth nations will be in dismay, perplexed by the roaring of the sea and the waves. People will die of fright in anticipation of what is coming upon the world, for the powers of the heavens will be shaken. And then they will see the Son of Man coming in a cloud with power and great glory. But when these signs begin to happen, stand erect and raise your heads because your redemption is at hand.

"Beware that your hearts do not become drowsy from carousing and drunkenness and the anxieties of daily life, and that day catch you by surprise like a trap. For that day will assault everyone who lives on the face of the earth. Be vigilant at all times and pray that you have strength to escape the tribulations that are imminent and to stand before the Son of Man."

Sunday

OPENING PRAYER

Lord Jesus,
Master of both the light and the darkness,
send your Holy Spirit upon our
preparations for Christmas.
We who have so much to do seek quiet
spaces to hear your voice each day.
We who are anxious over many things look
forward to your coming among us.
We who are blessed in so many ways long
for the complete joy of your kingdom.
We whose hearts are heavy seek the joy of
your presence.
We are your people, walking in darkness,
yet seeking the light.
To you we say, "Come, Lord Jesus!" Amen.

—The Advent Prayer by Henri Nouwen

LECTIO DIVINA ✎ SACRED READING OF SCRIPTURE

Feel free to take notes on the video reflection in the space below.

LECTIO DIVINA ✎ MEDITATION

The Gospel reading for this Sunday can be somewhat frightening since it contains images that we usually associate with the "end of the world."

How did the Old Testament use these images of the sun and moon darkening and the stars falling from the sky? What did this apocalyptic imagery describe?

Edward Sri says that one of the temptations we face if we hear the message of today's Gospel in terms of doom and gloom is that we can become discouraged and lose heart. However, God repeatedly tells us to "fear not."

What do people tend to get the most worried and discouraged about during this season?

Why do you think this is?

How can today's Gospel reading instill hope in Christ's followers, particularly during this Advent season?

What can you do to create a feeling of hope in your own life and in your family?

LECTIO DIVINA PRAYER & RESOLUTION

PRAYER: **Prayerfully consider the deepest worries and fears you carry in your heart. What are you most anxious about? Maybe it's something at work or in your family. Maybe it's a health or financial situation. In prayer, tell Jesus about your worries. Then imagine Jesus speaking to you the words from today's Gospel reading about him coming "in a cloud with power and great glory"—an image that reminds us that God is in control and he will come to set all things right. How might these words be a source of comfort for you in your troubles?**

RESOLUTION: **Reflect on one way you can live a more hope-filled existence this Advent season. Perhaps you need to trust more in God's goodness in your life, or maybe you need to make more time for prayer amidst the busyness of the season.**

Write down your thoughts, reflections, and your resolutions.

"He loves, he hopes, he waits. If he came down on our altars on certain days only, some sinner, on being moved to repentance, might have to look for him, and not finding him, might have to wait. Our Lord prefers to wait himself for the sinner for years rather than keep him waiting one instant." —St. Peter Julian Eymard

Monday

What are you hoping for during this season of waiting? Turn your concerns over to Jesus with the confident expectation that he will hear and answer you.

"It is the beautiful task of Advent to awaken in all of us memories of goodness and thus open doors of hope."—Cardinal Joseph Ratzinger (1986)

Tuesday

The first reading from the prophet Jeremiah speaks of a God who will fulfill all the promises he made to his children (see Jeremiah 33:14-16). Do you trust that God is a God who keeps his promises and who opens doors of hope? What areas of life are you afraid to turn over to God?

"Advent, like its cousin Lent, is a season for prayer and reformation of our hearts."
—Edward Hays, *A Pilgrim's Almanac*

Wednesday

Slowly pray the words of this week's psalm, reflecting in a special way on the phrase "guide me in your truth and teach me" (see Psalm 25:4-5, 8-9, 10, 14). Ask Jesus for the grace to seek after his truth through his guidance and grace.

What are some specific ways you need to be guided in his truth?

"Let your religion be less of a theory and more of a love affair."
—G.K. Chesterton

Thursday

Reread the second reading from St. Paul to the Thessalonians (see 1 Thessalonians 3:12–4:2). What does it mean to you to conduct yourself in a way that is pleasing to God? How can you change your daily habits so as to "strengthen your heart"?

"Somebody should tell us, right at the start of our lives, that we are dying. Then we might live life to the limit, every minute of every day. Do it! I say. Whatever you want to do, do it now! There are only so many tomorrows."
—Pope Paul VI

Friday

Reflect on Christ's message of hope from this week's Gospel Reading (see Luke 21:25-28, 34-36). What gives you hope in the midst of your trials? How often do you pray for the strength to escape or persevere in your tribulations?

"It is necessary to understand

that the whole of our life must be an 'advent,' a vigilant awaiting of the final coming of Christ… therefore, advent is, so to speak, an intense training that directs us decisively toward him who already came, who will come, and who comes continuously."

—Blessed John Paul II

Saturday

Think back on how you celebrated this first week of Advent. Was it centered in prayer? Was it rooted in hope? What one thing can you do right now, today, to make sure that this Advent is truly a new beginning?

"Learn the heart of God from the Word of God."—Pope St. Gregory

2ND SUNDAY OF ADVENT
~ YEAR C ~

MAKING STRAIGHT THE PATH OF THE LORD

READINGS FOR THE SECOND SUNDAY OF ADVENT

FIRST READING
- Baruch 5:1-9 -

Jerusalem, take off your robe of mourning and misery; / put on the splendor of glory from God forever: / wrapped in the cloak of justice from God, / bear on your head the mitre that displays the glory of the eternal name. / For God will show all the earth your splendor: / you will be named by God forever/ the peace of justice, the glory of God's worship.

Up, Jerusalem! Stand upon the heights; / look to the east and see your children / gathered from the east and the west / at the word of the Holy One, / rejoicing that they are remembered by God. / Led away on foot by their enemies they left you: / but God will bring them back to you / borne aloft in glory as on royal thrones. / For God has commanded / that every lofty mountain be made low, / and that the age-old depths and gorges / be filled to level ground, / that Israel may advance secure in the glory of God. / The forests and every fragrant kind of tree / have overshadowed Israel at God's command; / for God is leading Israel in joy / by the light of his glory, / with his mercy and justice for company.

RESPONSORIAL PSALM
- Psalm 126:1-2, 2-3, 4-5, 6 -

R: **The Lord has done great things for us; we are filled with joy.**

When the LORD brought back the captives of Zion,
we were like men dreaming.
Then our mouth was filled with laughter,
and our tongue with rejoicing.
R:

Then they said among the nations,
"The LORD has done great things for them."
The LORD has done great things for us;
we are glad indeed.
R:

Restore our fortunes, O LORD,
like the torrents in the southern desert.
Those who sow in tears
shall reap rejoicing.
R:

Although they go forth weeping,
carrying the seed to be sown,
they shall come back rejoicing,
carrying their sheaves.
R:

SECOND READING
- Philippians 1:4-6, 8-11 -

Brothers and sisters: I pray always with joy in my every prayer for all of you, because of your partnership for the gospel from the first day until now. I am confident of this, that the one who began a good work in you will continue to complete it until the day of Christ Jesus... God is my witness, how I long for all of you with the affection of Christ Jesus. And this is my prayer: that your love may increase ever more and more knowledge and every kind of perception, to discern what is of value, so that you may be pure and blameless for the day of Christ, filled with the fruit of righteousness that comes through Jesus Christ for the glory and praise of God.

GOSPEL
- Luke 3:1-6 -

In the fifteenth year of the reign of Tiberius Caesar, when Pontius Pilate was governor of Judea, and Herod was tetrarch of Galilee, and his brother Philip tetrarch of the region of Ituraea and Trachonitis, and Lysanians was tetrarch of Abilene, during the high priesthood of Annas and Caiaphas, the word of God came to John the son of Zechariah in the desert. John went throughout the whole region of the Jordan, proclaiming a baptism of repentance for the forgiveness of sins, as it is written in the book of the words of the prophet Isaiah: A voice of one crying out in the desert: / "Prepare the way of the Lord, / make straight his paths. / Every valley shall be filled/ and every mountain and hill shall be made low. / The winding roads shall be made straight, / and the rough ways made smooth, / and all flesh shall see the salvation of God."

Sunday

OPENING PRAYER

You once favored, LORD, your land,
restored the captives of Jacob.
You forgave the guilt of your people,
pardoned all their sins.
You withdrew all your wrath,
turned back from your burning anger.

Restore us, God of our salvation;
let go of your displeasure with us.
Will you be angry with us forever,
prolong your anger for all generations?
Certainly you will again restore our life,
that your people may rejoice in you.
Show us, LORD, your mercy;
grant us your salvation. Amen.

—Psalm 85:1-7

LECTIO DIVINA ❧ SACRED READING OF SCRIPTURE

Feel free to take notes on the video reflection in the space below.

LECTIO DIVINA ❧ MEDITATION

Tim Gray talks about the difference between a physical return and a spiritual return. Returning physically is relatively easy, but how do we make a spiritual return?

How does recognition and confession of our sins begin to straighten the paths of our lives?

What are some ways in which you've experienced God's grace keeping you on a straight path in your life?

LECTIO DIVINA ❧ PRAYER & RESOLUTION

PRAYER: Reflect on the words from the Gospel reading about how the Lord is coming to make the winding roads straight. Ask Jesus what they mean in your own life. What roads in your life are winding—are not the right path? What rough areas need to be made smooth?

Take the word that comes to mind and reflect for a moment on what it means to you personally. For example, you might have been attracted to the words "winding road." Ask yourself what they mean in your own life. What roads are winding? How can you make them straight?

RESOLUTION: St. Augustine said, "God created us without us, but he did not will to save us without us." Ask God today what he wants you to do to prepare the way of the Lord in your heart. What practical thing can you do this week to straighten the paths of your life?

"When the Church celebrates the liturgy of Advent each year, she makes present this ancient expectancy of the Messiah, for by sharing in the long preparation for the Savior's first coming, the faithful renew their ardent desire for his second coming." —CCC 524*

* 524 Cf. Rev. 22:17

Monday

Last Sunday's Gospel reading from Luke 3:1-6 talks about preparing the way of the Lord and making straight his path. In your prayer today, ask God how he is calling you to make straight your ways this Advent. How can you prepare the way for him in your daily life (for example, in interactions with family members, in the workplace, in your parish)?

"Our Lord himself I saw in this venerable Sacrament [of Confession] ... I felt as if my chains fell, as those of St. Peter at the touch of the Divine messenger. My God, what new scenes for my soul!"

—St. Elizabeth Ann Seton

Tuesday

Reread last Sunday's first reading from Baruch 5:1-9. Israel is told to take off her cloak of mourning and misery when she returns from exile. How is our return from sin a time that we can take off our mourning and misery? Journal about how you feel when you have experienced the Sacrament of Confession. Do you feel as if "chains" have fallen from your soul?

If you have not yet experienced the Sacrament of Confession, how would this reading help you to better prepare for the Sacrament?

"Lord what wilt thou have me do? Behold the true sign of a totally perfect soul: when one has reached the point of giving up his will so completely that he no longer seeks, expects, or desires to do ought but that which God wills." —St. Bernard of Clairvoux

Wednesday

In last Sunday's second reading, Philippians 1:4-6, 8-11, St. Paul says: "The one who began a good work in you will continue to complete it until the day of Christ Jesus." What good works do you see in yourself? What works would you like to see continue to grow, especially during this Advent season?

"O my children, how great is Divine Providence! How generous God is to us! How much he loves us! Let us always be grateful and good!"

—St. John Bosco

Thursday

The responsorial psalm for last Sunday includes the verse "The Lord has done great things for us;/ Oh, how happy we were!" (Psalm 126:3). Take some time in prayer to list at least five things you are grateful for today. List them in your journal and add to them as you think of more ways God has been generous to you.

"Trust in the LORD with all your heart,/ on your own intelligence rely not;/ In all your ways be mindful of him,/ and he will make straight your paths." —Proverbs 3:5-6

Friday

Both the first reading (Baruch 5:1-9) and the Gospel reading (Luke 3:1-6) from last Sunday talk about mountains being made low and valleys being filled in to make a straight path. What mountains or valleys do you need cleared this week to make a clear path for you to follow? How does trusting the Lord enable you to make a straight path in your life? What areas are the most difficult to entrust to God? Family? Health? Finances?

"You changed my mourning into dancing; / you took off my sackcloth / and clothed me with gladness. / So that my glory may praise you / and not be silent. O LORD, my God, / forever will I give you thanks."—Psalm 30:12-13

Saturday

In last Sunday's responsorial psalm we heard the verse "Those who sow in tears/ will reap with cries of joy" (Psalm 126:5). What sorrow in your life right now (or in the life of someone you know) do you need God to turn into joy? Bring it to him in prayer today, trusting that he loves you and will indeed fill you with gladness.

"This is the month, and this the happy morn, Wherein the Son of Heaven's eternal King, Of wedded maid and virgin mother born, Our great redemption from above did bring, For so the holy sages once did sing, That he our deadly forfeit should release, And with his Father work us a perpetual peace." —John Milton

3RD SUNDAY OF ADVENT
❧ YEAR C ❧

INVITATION TO JOY

READINGS FOR THE
THIRD SUNDAY OF ADVENT

FIRST READING
- Zephaniah 3:14-18 -

Shout for joy, O daughter Zion! / Sing joyfully, O Israel! / Be glad and exult with all your heart, / O daughter Jerusalem! / The LORD has removed the judgment against you / he has turned away your enemies; / the King of Israel, the LORD, is in your midst, / you have no further misfortune to fear. / On that day, it shall be said to Jerusalem: / Fear not, O Zion, be not discouraged! / The LORD, your God, is in your midst, / a mighty savior; / he will rejoice over you with gladness, / and renew you in his love, / he will sing joyfully because of you, / as one sings at festivals.

RESPONSORIAL PSALM
- Isaiah 12: 2-3, 4, 5-6 -

R: **Cry out with joy and gladness: for among you
is the great and Holy One of Israel.**

God indeed is my savior;
I am confident and unafraid.
My strength and my courage is the LORD,
and he has been my savior.
With joy you will draw water
at the fountain of salvation.
R:
Give thanks to the LORD, acclaim his name;
among the nations make known his deeds,
proclaim how exalted is his name.
R:
Sing praise to the LORD for his glorious achievement;
let this be known throughout all the earth.
Shout with exultation, O city of Zion,
for great in your midst
is the Holy One of Israel!
R:

SECOND READING
- Philippians 4:4-7 -

Brothers and sisters: Rejoice in the Lord always. I shall say it again: rejoice! Your kindness should be known to all. The Lord is near. Have no anxiety at all, but in everything, by prayer and petition, with thanksgiving, make your requests known to God. Then the peace of God that surpasses all understanding will guard your hearts and minds in Christ Jesus.

GOSPEL
- Luke 3:10-18 -

The crowds asked John the Baptist, "What should we do?" He said to them in reply, "Whoever has two cloaks should share with the person who has none. And whoever has food should do likewise." Even tax collectors came to be baptized and they said to him, "Teacher, what should we do?" He answered them, "Stop collecting more than what is prescribed." Soldiers also asked him, "And what is it that we should do?" He told them, "Do not practice extortion, do not falsely accuse anyone, and be satisfied with your wages."

Now the people were filled with expectation, and all were asking in their hearts whether John might be the Christ. John answered them all, saying, "I am baptizing you with water, but one mightier than I is coming. I am not worthy to loosen the thongs of his sandals. He will baptize you with the Holy Spirit and fire. His winnowing fan is in his hand to clear his threshing floor and to gather the wheat into his barn, but the chaff he will burn with unquenchable fire." Exhorting them in many other ways, he preached good news to the people.

Sunday

OPENING PRAYER

Let the heavens be glad and the earth rejoice;
let the sea and what fills it resound;
let the plains be joyful and all that is in them.
Then let the trees of the forest rejoice
before the Lord who comes,
who comes to govern the earth,
To govern the world with justice
and the peoples with faithfulness. Amen.

—Psalm 96:11-13

LECTIO DIVINA ❧ SACRED READING OF SCRIPTURE

Feel free to take notes on the video reflection in the space below.

LECTIO DIVINA ❧ MEDITATION

John the Baptist preached and performed a baptism of repentance that foreshadowed the Sacrament of Baptism. What does Baptism mean to you? How does the season of Advent call us to live out or prepare for our baptismal promises more faithfully?

What are some differences between the emotion of happiness and Christian joy? How can we maintain joy in our lives even in the face of sorrow or hardship? Do you have an example of a time when you were able to rejoice even when you didn't feel happy?

29

LECTIO DIVINA ✿ PRAYER & RESOLUTION

PRAYER: Prayerfully place yourself in today's Gospel reading. Picture yourself on the bank of the Jordan River listening to John's announcement that the Messiah is finally coming. Imagine the joy you and many of the others in the crowd would have hearing that the Messiah will finally be arriving after hundreds of years of waiting. Imagine John the Baptist saying to you, "Repent, for the Kingdom of heaven is at hand." How does this call to repentance make you feel? Are you excited? scared?

RESOLUTION: Imagine hearing the John the Baptist's instructions to the crowds to practice charity and justice in their daily lives. What might John tell you specifically to do to put your life in order in preparation for the coming of the Lord? What is one thing you can do this week in order to make your daily life a greater witness to Jesus?

"This is the day the Lord has made, / let us rejoice in it and be glad."
—Psalm 118:24

Monday

In Sunday's first reading, the prophet Zephaniah says, "The LORD, your God, is in your midst,/ a mighty savior;/ he will rejoice over you with gladness,/ and renew you in his love,/ he will sing joyfully because of you" (Zephaniah 3:17). Is it easy or difficult for you to believe that God rejoices over you? Why? Take some time today to ask God to help you feel his presence and rest securely in the knowledge of his love for you.

"God never ceases to draw man to himself." —CCC 27

Tuesday

The readings from Sunday emphasize God's presence with his people: "The LORD, your God, is in your midst" (Zephaniah 3:17); "Great in your midst/ is the Holy One of Israel!" (Isaiah 12:6); and "The Lord is near" (Philippians 4:5). Take some time to read and think about how these verses can make you feel more joyful and secure in God's love. Note ways that God makes you aware of his presence this week. Ask God for the grace to be more aware of his nearness.

"You, LORD, are near to all who call upon you, / to all who call upon you in truth." —Psalm 145:18

Wednesday

Read Philippians 4:4-7. Think about what St. Paul says about rejoicing, anxiety, and peace. Which of these three states of being best describes you right now? What are you anxious about and what does Paul suggest you do? Spend some time in prayer entrusting these to God.

"Jesus' prayer, characterized by thanksgiving, reveals to us how to ask: before the gift is given, Jesus commits himself to the One who in giving gives himself. The Giver is more precious than the gift; he is the 'treasure'; in him abides his Son's heart; the gift is given 'as well.' "

—CCC 2604

Thursday

In last Sunday's Gospel reading, John the Baptist instructed the crowd, tax collectors, and soldiers on ways that they could put their lives in order to prepare for God's salvation. What do you think he would say to you? List three things that you can do this week to help prepare for the coming of the Savior.

"Do not lose courage in considering your own imperfections, but instantly set about remedying them." —St. Francis de Sales

Friday

Consider the following verse from last Sunday's second reading from Philippians: "Then the peace of God that surpasses all understanding will guard your hearts and minds in Christ Jesus" (Philippians 4:7). Have you ever experienced the peace of God? What did it feel like? When did you feel it? If you have never felt God's peace, ask God to show you what you need to do to be receptive.

"May today there be peace within. May you trust God that you are exactly where you are meant to be."

—St. Theresa of Lisieux

Saturday

This past week may have been filled with busyness, but the Church tells us that it is a time for joy as well. In what ways have you experienced joy this Advent? In your prayer time, reflect on how you might experience less anxiety and more joy. Write down three things that you are grateful for this week.

"You ask me whether I am in good spirits. How could I not be so? As long as Faith gives me strength I will always be joyful. Sadness ought to be banished from Catholic souls... the purpose for which we have been created shows us the path; even if strewn with many thorns, it is not a sad path. It is joyful even in the face of sorrow." —Blessed Pier Giorgio Frassati

4TH SUNDAY OF ADVENT
❧ YEAR C ❧

SERVICE AND HUMILITY

READINGS FOR THE
FOURTH SUNDAY OF ADVENT

FIRST READING
- Micah 5:1-4 -

Thus says the LORD:/ You, Bethlehem-Ephrathah/ too small to be among the clans of Judah,/ from you shall come forth for me/ one who is to be ruler in Israel;/ whose origin is from of old,/ from ancient times./ Therefore the Lord will give them up, until the time/ when she who is to give birth has borne,/ and the rest of kindred shall return/ to the children of Israel./ He shall stand firm and shepherd his flock/ by the strength of the Lord,/ in the majestic name of the LORD, his God;/ and they shall remain, for now his greatness/ shall reach to the ends of the earth;/ he shall be peace.

RESPONSORIAL PSALM
- Psalm 80:2-3, 15-16, 18-19 -

R: **Lord, make us turn to you; let us see your face
and we shall be saved.**

O shepherd of Israel, hearken,
from your throne upon the cherubim, shine forth.
Rouse your power,
and come to save us.
R:

Once again, O LORD of hosts,
look down from heaven, and see;
take care of this vine,
and protect what your right hand has planted,
the son of man whom you yourself made strong.
R:

May your help be with the man of your right hand,
with the son of man whom you yourself made strong.
Then we will no more withdraw from you;
give us new life, and we will call upon your name.
R:

SECOND READING

- Hebrews 10:5-10 -

Brothers and sisters: When Christ came into the world, he said: "Sacrifice and offering you did not desire, but a body you prepared for me; in holocausts and sin offerings you took no delight. Then I said, 'As is written of me in the scroll, behold, I come to do your will, O God.'

First he says, "Sacrifices and offerings, holocausts and sin offerings, you neither desired nor delighted in." These are offered according to the law. Then he says, "Behold, I come to do your will." He takes away the first to establish the second. By this "will," we have been consecrated through the offering of the body of Jesus Christ once for all.

GOSPEL

- Luke 1:39-45 -

Mary set out and traveled to the hill country in haste to a town of Judah, where she entered the house of Zechariah and greeted Elizabeth. When Elizabeth heard Mary's greeting, the infant leaped in her womb, and Elizabeth, filled with the Holy Spirit, cried out in a loud voice and said, "Blessed are you among woman, and blessed is the fruit of your womb. And how does this happen to me, that the mother of my Lord should come to me? For at the moment the sound of your greeting reached my ears, the infant in my womb leaped for joy. Blessed are you who believed that what was spoken to you by the Lord would be fulfilled."

Sunday

OPENING PRAYER

How numerous, O LORD, my God,
you have made your wondrous deeds!
And in your plans for us there is none to equal you.
Should I wish to declare or tell them,
too many are they to recount.
Sacrifice and offering you do not want;
but ears open to obedience you gave me.
Holocausts and sin-offerings you do not require;
so I said, "Here I am;
your commands for me are written in the scroll.
To do your will is my delight;
my God, your law is in my heart!" —Psalm 40: 6-9

Grant us, O Lord, an open ear to hear your Word,
to take it to heart, and to act on it.
May we delight to do your will,
as you plant your law more and more deeply
within our hearts. Amen.

LECTIO DIVINA ❧ SACRED READING OF SCRIPTURE

Feel free to take notes on the video reflection in the space below.

LECTIO DIVINA ❧ MEDITATION

In the Visitation Mary gives us a profound example of humility and service. Why do you think that Mary went to help Elizabeth?

What are some ways you can be of service to your family this last week of Advent?

Humility has been defined as "seeing your place and taking it."
Before you watched this video, how would you have explained humility?

What is the "place" in which you find yourself in life right now?

How does your attitude about your place in life match the definitions of humility that we have been discussing?

How would you recognize the movement of the Holy Spirit calling you to humility in your own life?

What would be some of the characteristics of his activity?

LECTIO DIVINA ✺ PRAYER & RESOLUTION

PRAYER: Imagine that you are one of Elizabeth's neighbors. You are at the well, drawing water for the day, when you see Mary, Elizabeth's cousin, coming towards you on the road. You listen as Elizabeth greets Mary and exclaims, "How is it that the mother of my Lord should come to me?" You then realize that Mary is with child and is carrying the Lord himself in her womb! How do you feel knowing that the Lord is in your midst and has come to us even as a baby in the womb of Mary? What does this tell us about God's love for us?

RESOLUTION: This week, take some time to reflect upon the reality that the Son of God became a baby and was really carried in Mary's womb. Use your journal to write down your thoughts and reflections. What can you do this week to become Christ's loving and humble presence to others?

"Hannah also prayed and said, 'My heart exults in the LORD; my strength is exalted in the LORD ... because I rejoice in thy salvation.'"
—1 Samuel 2:1 (RSV)

Monday

Sunday's first reading from Micah begins with an address to the city of Bethlehem-Ephrathah as being too small to be of much notice, yet from it is to come the Messiah. The Lord can bring great things out of humble, unnoticed sources. Think of an event in your life that, while seeming insignificant at the time, God used to make an enormous difference. What were some of the spiritual effects of that event? Reflect on how your life would have been different without that event.

"God resists the proud, / but gives grace to the humble." —James 4:6

Tuesday

Elizabeth said that she felt her child leap for joy when Mary approached. Can you recall a time when you leapt for joy? What brings you the most joy this time of year?

"We must say, 'I belong to you. You can do whatever you like.' And this is our strength. This is the joy of the Lord."
—Blessed Teresa of Calcutta

Wednesday

In the second of Sunday's readings, the author of Hebrews quotes Psalm 40 to the effect that God has not taken any delight in the various kinds of sacrifices offered according to the Law, but only when we say, "I come to do your will, O God." How do you know God's will for your life? How can you do God's will this week?

"A wise lover values not so much the gift of the lover as the love of the giver."

—Thomas á Kempis

Thursday

In our study we learned how Mary came to serve and how Elizabeth expressed humility at their meeting. One thing they had in common was that they needed to trust God in their situations. Do you find it easy or hard to trust God? Write about one area in your life where you need to have greater trust in God.

"Woe to timid hearts and to slack hands, and to the sinner who walks along two ways! Woe to the faint heart, for it has no trust! Therefore it will not be sheltered." —Sirach 2:12-13 (RSV)

Friday

The video last Sunday referred to the many concerns that Mary had on her mind even as she decided to go "to the hill country in haste" to visit Elizabeth. Using your imagination, make a list in your journal of some of the concerns she may have had. How do you think Mary dealt with her concerns? How do you deal with similar concerns in your own life?

Saturday

Having recognized Mary as "the mother of my Lord," Elizabeth wonders at the thought that the "mother of my Lord should come to me." In your journal, reflect on a time when the wonder of God's presence struck you, and what it meant to you. If you cannot recall such a time, write a short prayer asking the Holy Spirit to help you recognize his presence.

"And David was afraid of the LORD that day, and he said, 'How can the ark of the LORD come to me?'" —2 Samuel 6:9 (RSV)

THE HOLY FAMILY OF JESUS, MARY, AND JOSEPH

SUNDAY WITHIN THE OCTAVE OF CHRISTMAS
❧ YEAR C ❧

WAITING ON GOD'S ANSWER

READINGS FOR THE SUNDAY WITHIN THE OCTAVE OF CHRISTMAS

FIRST READING
- 1 Samuel 1:20-22, 24-28 -

In those days Hannah conceived, and at the end of her term bore a son whom she called Samuel, since she had asked the LORD for him. The next time her husband Elkanah was going up with the rest of his household to offer the customary sacrifice to the LORD and to fulfill his vows, Hannah did not go, explaining to her husband, "Once the child is weaned, I will take him to appear before the LORD and to remain there forever; I will offer him as a perpetual nazirite."

Once Samuel was weaned, Hannah brought him up with her, along with a three-year-old bull, an ephah of flour, and a skin of wine, and presented him at the temple of the LORD in Shiloh. After the boy's father had sacrificed the young bull, Hannah, his mother, approached Eli and said: "Pardon, my lord! As you live my lord, I am the woman who stood near you here, praying to the LORD. I prayed for this child, and the LORD granted my request. Now I, in turn, give him to the LORD; as long as he lives, he shall be dedicated to the LORD." Hannah left Samuel there.

RESPONSORIAL PSALM
- Psalm:84:2-3, 5-6, 9-10 -

R: **Blessed are they who dwell in your house, O Lord!**

How lovely is your dwelling place, O LORD of hosts!
My soul yearns and pines for the courts of the LORD.
My heart and flesh cry out for the living God.
R:

Happy are those who dwell in your house!
Continually they praise you.
Happy the men whose strength you are!
Their hearts are set upon the pilgrimage.
R:

O LORD of hosts, hear my prayer;
hearken, O God of Jacob!
O God, behold our shield;
and look upon the face of your anointed.
R:

SECOND READING

- 1 John 3:1-2, 21-24 -

See what love the Father has bestowed on us that we may be called the children of God. And so we are. The reason the world does not know us is that it did not know him. Beloved, we are God's children now; what we shall be has not yet been revealed. We do know that when it is revealed we shall be like him, for we shall see him as he is.

Beloved, if our hearts do not condemn us, we have confidence in God and receive from him whatever we ask, because we keep his commandments and do what pleases him. And his commandment is this: we should believe in the name of his Son, Jesus Christ, and love one another just as he commanded us. Those who keep his commandments remain in him, and he in them, and the way we know that he remains in us is from the Spirit that he gave us.

GOSPEL

- Luke 2:41-52 -

Each year Jesus' parents went to Jerusalem for the feast of Passover, and when he was twelve years old, they went up according to festival custom. After they had completed its days, as they were returning, the boy Jesus remained behind in Jerusalem, but his parents did not know it. Thinking that he was in the caravan, they journeyed for a day and looked for him among their relatives and acquaintances, but not finding him, they returned to Jerusalem to look for him. After three days they found him in the temple, sitting in the midst of the teachers, listening to them and asking questions, and all who heard him were astounded at his understanding and his answers. When his parents saw him, they were astonished, and his mother said to him, "Son, why have you done this to us? Your father and I have been looking for you with great anxiety." And he said to them, "Why were you looking for me? Did you not know that I must be in my Father's house?" But they did not understand what he said to them. He went down with them and came to Nazareth, and was obedient to them; and his mother kept all these things in her heart. And Jesus advanced in wisdom and age and favor before God and man.

Sunday

OPENING PRAYER

O Light of the World, Infinite God, Father of Eternity, Giver of Wisdom and Knowledge, and ineffable dispenser of every spiritual grace; who knows all things before they are made, who makes the darkness and the light; put forth thy hand and touch my mouth, and make it as a sharp sword to utter eloquently thy words.

Make my tongue, Oh Lord, as a chosen arrow, to declare faithfully thy wonders.

Put thy Spirit, Oh Lord, in my heart that I may perceive; in my soul, that I may retain; and in my conscience, that I may meditate.

Do thou lovingly, holily, mercifully, clemently, and gently inspire me with thy grace. Do thou teach, guide, and strengthen the comings in and goings out of my senses and my thoughts.

And let thy discipline instruct me even to the end, and the Counsel of the Most High help me through thy infinite wisdom and mercy. Amen.

—Prayer for Wisdom by St. Anthony of Padua

LECTIO DIVINA ❧ SACRED READING OF SCRIPTURE

Feel free to take notes on the video reflection in the space below.

LECTIO DIVINA ❧ MEDITATION

Sometimes it is part of God's plan to allow us to wander lost or be afraid, so that we can learn to rise above our trials.

What does it mean to you to "rise above your trials"?

How might Mary and Joseph be an example of this?

The Finding in the Temple started out as a time of anxiety but ended up in joy and recognition of God's providence.

Share a time in your life that began in fear but concluded with a deeper appreciation and understanding of God's work in your life.

LECTIO DIVINA ✺ PRAYER & RESOLUTION

PRAYER: Put yourself in today's Gospel scene and imagine going with Mary throughout Jerusalem for three days looking for the child Jesus. You finally go with her into the Temple and are surprised to see Jesus talking with the teachers there while Mary and Joseph have been anxiously searching for him these last 72 hours. What is your reaction? You listen as he and Mary talk and you hear him tell her that he had to be in his Father's house, doing his Father's work. What do you think Jesus means by this?

RESOLUTION: In what ways might you feel you have "lost" Jesus? Take a moment now to reflect on an area in your life where you are seeking Jesus' help in your life but do not seem able to find it. Maybe you are searching for an answer or a solution to a difficult problem. Perhaps you are in need of his healing and power. Or maybe you simply long to be with him in prayer but do not sense his closeness. Prayerfully consider how, even though you have not found the clarity, spiritual strength, or sense of intimacy with Jesus that you have been looking for, Jesus might be working in your life right now, doing his Father's work in the temple of your soul. What would that mean to you? This week, when you face a difficult situation, remember that Jesus is always available to you, always doing his Father's work in the temple of your soul, even if he seems "lost" to you.

"Let nothing disturb you, Let nothing frighten you, All things are passing away: God never changes. Patience obtains all things. Whoever has God lacks nothing; God alone suffices."
—St. Teresa of Avila

Monday

Write down one thing that is worrying or concerning you. Ask Jesus to help you let go of your anxiety and trust that God will answer your prayers.

"Even though I walk through the valley of the shadow of death, I fear no evil, for thou art with me; thy rod and thy staff, they comfort me." —Psalm 23:4 (RSV)

Tuesday

In the first reading, Hannah says that her son, Samuel, was the direct answer to her prayer for a child. This week keep track of your prayers and see how God answers you in your life.

"O Lord, we ask for a boundless confidence and trust in your divine mercy, and the courage to accept the crosses and sufferings which bring immense goodness to our souls and that of your Church." —Padre Pio

Wednesday

The psalm says, "Lord of hosts, hear my prayer." Why do you think we ask God to hear our prayer? Is it because God isn't listening, or is it because we need to remind ourselves that God is always listening? Explore whatever thoughts come up when you think about how God answers prayer.

"Do not lose courage in considering your own imperfections."

—Saint Francis de Sales

Thursday

In the second reading, John says: "We have confidence in God and receive from him whatever we ask, because we keep his commandments and do what pleases him. And his commandment is this: we should believe in the name of his Son, Jesus Christ, and love one another just as he commanded us." Are you keeping God's commandments? Do you believe in the name of Jesus and love others? How can you be more faithful in this regard?

"Today, even in this modern age marked by anxiety and uncertainty, we live the event of the Resurrection, which changed the face of our life and changed the history of humanity." —Pope Benedict XVI

Friday

Even though Mary was the Mother of God, she still didn't know everything about God's plan and had to accept the unfolding of her life on faith, just as we do. How does understanding this about Mary help you with your own daily journey?

"Worry does not empty tomorrow of its sorrow; it empties today of its strength."
—Corrie ten Boom, twentieth-century Dutch evangelist

Saturday

Now that the new year has started, what can you do to learn to trust God's guidance and protection more this year? List at least three areas of your life that you can start to turn over to God.

"Have no anxiety about anything, but in everything by prayer and supplication with thanksgiving let your requests be made known to God." —Philippians 4:6 (RSV)

THE EPIPHANY
OF OUR LORD
❧ YEAR C ❧

GIFTS FOR
THE KING

READINGS FOR THE EPIPHANY OF OUR LORD

FIRST READING
- Isaiah 60:1-6 -

Rise up in splendor, Jerusalem! Your light has come,/ the glory of the Lord shines upon you./ See, darkness covers the earth,/ and thick clouds cover the peoples;/ but upon you the Lord shines,/ and over you appears his glory./ Nations shall walk by your light,/ and kings by your shining radiance./ Raise your eyes and look about;/ they all gather and come to you:/ your sons come from afar,/ and your daughters in the arms of their nurses.

Then you shall be radiant at what you see,/ your heart shall throb and overflow,/ for the riches of the sea shall be emptied out before you,/ the wealth of nations shall be brought to you./ Caravans of camels shall fill you,/ dromedaries from Midian and Ephah;/ all from Sheba shall come/ bearing gold and frankincense,/ and proclaiming the praises of the Lord.

RESPONSORIAL PSALM
- Psalm 72:1-2, 7-8, 10-11, 12-13 -

R: **Lord, every nation on earth will adore you.**

O God, with your judgment endow the king,
and with your justice, the king's son;
he shall govern your people with justice
and your afflicted ones with judgment.
R:

Justice shall flourish in his days,
and profound peace, till the moon be no more.
May he rule from sea to sea,
and from the River to the ends of the earth.
R:

The kings of Tarshish and the Isles shall offer gifts;
the kings of Arabia and Seba shall bring tribute.
All kings shall pay him homage,
all nations shall serve him.
R:

For he shall rescue the poor when he cries out,
and the afflicted when he has no one to help him.
He shall have pity for the lowly and the poor;
the lives of the poor he shall save.
R:

SECOND READING
- Ephesians 3:2-3, 5-6 -

Brothers and sisters: You have heard of the stewardship of God's grace that was given to me for your benefit, namely, that the mystery was made known to me by revelation ... It was not made known to people in other generations as it has now been revealed to his holy apostles and prophets by the Spirit: that the Gentiles are coheirs, members of the same body, and copartners in the promise in Christ Jesus through the gospel.

GOSPEL
- Matthew 2:2-12 -

When Jesus was born in Bethlehem of Judea, in days of King Herod, behold, magi from the east arrived Jerusalem, saying, "Where is the newborn king of the Jews? We saw his star at its rising and have come to do him homage." When King Herod heard this, he was greatly troubled, and all Jerusalem with him. Assembling all the chief priests and the scribes of the people, he inquired of them where the Christ was to be born. They said to him, "In Bethlehem of Judea, for thus it has been written through the prophet: And you, Bethlehem, land of Judah,/ are by no means least among the rulers of Judah;/ since from you shall come a ruler, who is to shepherd my people Israel."/ Then Herod called the magi secretly and ascertained from them the time of the star's appearance. He sent them to Bethlehem and said, "Go and search diligently for the child. When you have found him, bring me word, that I too may go and do him homage." After their audience with the king they set out. And behold, the star that they had seen at its rising preceded them, until it came and stopped over the place where the child was. They were overjoyed at seeing the star, and on entering the house they saw the child with Mary his mother. They prostrated themselves and did him homage. Then they opened their treasures and offered him gifts of gold, frankincense, and myrrh. And having been warned in a dream not to return to Herod, they departed for their country by another way.

Sunday

OPENING PRAYER

The heavens are shining with the clear beauty of the stars, O Lord, and the very earth is made beautiful by a shining light, because thou didst vouchsafe to appear to the world from out thy holy dwelling place. Remove, therefore, from our hearts all sadness, for unto this end art thou come, that thou mayest make all things new. Grant also that light unto our eyes which may purify us and fit us to behold thee forever; that thus we who preach to the nations the glad joys of thy Apparition, may be made glad with thee in infinite joy. Amen.

—Epiphany prayer from the *Mozarabic Breviary*
(an early breviary used in Spain).

LECTIO DIVINA ❧ SACRED READING OF SCRIPTURE

Feel free to take notes on the video reflection in the space below.

LECTIO DIVINA ❧ MEDITATION

In this week's reading, we hear about the Magi, wise men who came to visit the Messiah. Who were the Magi, and what do their three gifts signify?

How do the Magi's gifts of gold, frankincense, and myrrh shed light on the ways in which we offer our lives as a gift to Jesus?

Which of these do you feel is the hardest gift for you to offer, and why?

LECTIO DIVINA ✺ PRAYER & RESOLUTION

PRAYER: Prayerfully place yourself in today's Gospel reading. Imagine that you are with the Magi following the star to find the newborn king of the Jews. When you arrive at the humble house in Bethlehem and finally see the child Jesus with his parents, how do you feel? What do you say as you come forward to offer him a gift?

RESOLUTION: The Magi brought the precious and significant gifts of gold, frankincense, and myrrh to offer to Jesus. What gift can you give King Jesus this week? Perhaps you give him "gold" in the sense of accepting him as King in your life by living more according to his will? Or maybe you give him more "frankincense" in the sense of dedicating more time for prayer. Or you might want to offer him more "myrrh" in the sense of making sacrifices to serve others or uniting to him more in a particular suffering you are experiencing. In prayer with the Lord, choose one specific gift you could give to Jesus this week, and ask for the grace to carry out this resolution.

"In the context of the 'great mystery' of Christ and of the Church, all are called to respond—as a bride—with the gift of their lives to the inexpressible gift of the love of Christ, who alone, as the Redeemer of the world, is the Church's Bridegroom." —Blessed John Paul II

Monday

In last Sunday's Gospel reading from Matthew 2:2-12, the Magi follow the star to Jerusalem seeking the new king, but it is only when they consult the Scriptures that they are able to find the child Jesus in Bethlehem. How can you use the Scriptures to help you find your way to the Lord? In what areas in your life do you need to depend more on God's Word to direct you?

"All the troubles of the Church, all the evils in the world, flow from this source: that men do not by clear and sound knowledge and serious consideration penetrate into the truths of Sacred Scripture."

—St. Teresa of Avila

Tuesday

Reread last Sunday's first reading from Isaiah 60:1-6 in which the prophet says that the glory of the Lord shines upon you. How does it make you feel knowing that the Lord is casting his glory on you? How can you bring the radiance of God's glory to those around you this week?

"Let your door stand open to receive him, unlock your soul to him, offer him a welcome in your mind, and then you will see the riches of simplicity, the treasures of peace, the joy of grace. Throw wide the gate of your heart, stand before the sun of the everlasting light." —St. Ambrose

Wednesday

Last Sunday's responsorial psalm starts out with a request for wisdom: "O God, with your judgment endow the king,/ and with your justice, the king's son;/ he shall govern your people with justice/ and your afflicted ones with judgment" (Psalm 72:1-2). In what areas do you need God's help for right judgment this week? Remember that through Christ, you have the power of the Holy Spirit in your life. Take time in your prayer today to ask the Holy Spirit for his wisdom and guidance in areas where you are having a particular struggle.

"No one, whether shepherd or wise man, can approach God here below except by kneeling before the manger at Bethlehem and adoring him hidden in the weakness of a newborn child." —CCC 563

Thursday

Reread last Sunday's second reading in Ephesians 3:2-3, 5-6 where it says that we, the Gentiles, are now "coheirs, members of the same body, and copartners in the promise in Christ Jesus through the gospel." What does this mean to you? What affect does knowing that you are now among God's chosen people have on your everyday life?

"God has created me to do him some definite service; he has committed some work to me which he has not committed to another. I have my mission—I may never know it in this life, but I shall be told it in the next...I have a part in this great work; I am a link in a chain, a bond of connection between persons." —Blessed John Henry Newman

Friday

In last Sunday's responsorial psalm we hear that the king "shall rescue the poor when he cries out, and the afflicted when he has no one to help him. He shall have pity for the lowly and the poor; the lives of the poor he shall save." Who do you know who might be considered poor, either economically or spiritually? Lift them up in prayer this week while, at the same time, asking God to extend his mercy and pity to you as well.

"If you want God to hear your prayers, hear the voice of the poor. If you wish God to anticipate your wants, provide those of the needy without waiting for them to ask you. Especially anticipate the needs of those who are ashamed to beg. To make them ask for alms is to make them buy it."

—St. Thomas of Villanova

Saturday

In last Sunday's second reading, Ephesians 3:2-3, 5-6, St. Paul talks about how the mystery has been made known to us by the Spirit in a way it was not made known to previous generations: "It has now been revealed (emphasis added) to his holy apostles and prophets by the Spirit." Consider what it means for something to be "revealed." What is the mystery that Paul is talking about? (Hint: that we are now co-heirs to the promise in Christ.) How has that mystery been revealed to you?

"We must open our eyes to admire God who hides and at the same time reveals himself in things and introduces us into the realms of mystery... we must be pure and simple like children, capable of admiring, being astonished, of marveling, and being enchanted by the divine gestures of love and closeness we witness."—Pope John Paul II

THE BAPTISM OF THE LORD

1ST SUNDAY
IN ORDINARY TIME
❧ YEAR C ❧

CHRIST'S BAPTISM
AND OUR OWN

READINGS FOR THE FIRST SUNDAY IN ORDINARY TIME

FIRST READING
- Isaiah 40:1-5, 9-11 -

Comfort, give comfort to my people,/ says your God./ Speak tenderly to Jerusalem,/ and proclaim to her/ that her service is at an end,/ her guilt is expiated;/ indeed, she has received from the hand of the Lord/ double for all her sins.

A voice cries out:/ In the desert prepare the way of the Lord!/ Make straight in the wasteland a highway for our God!/ Every valley shall be filled in,/ every mountain and hill shall be made low;/ the rugged land shall be made plain,/ the rough country, a broad valley./ Then the glory of the Lord shall be revealed,/ and all people shall see it together;/ for the mouth of the Lord has spoken.

Go up onto a high mountain,/ Zion, herald of glad tidings;/ cry out at the top of your voice,/ Jerusalem, herald of goods news!/ Fear not to cry out/ and say to the cities of Judah:/ Here is your God!/ Here comes with power/ the Lord God,/ who rules by a strong arm;/ here is his reward with him,/ his recompense before him./ Like a shepherd he feeds his flock;/ in his arms he gathers the lambs,/ carrying them in his bosom,/ and leading the ewes with care.

RESPONSORIAL PSALM
- Psalm 104:1b-2, 3-4, 24-25, 27-28, 29-30 -

R: **O bless the Lord, my soul.**

O Lord, my God, you are great indeed!
You are clothed with majesty and glory,
robed in light as with a cloak.
You have a spread out the heavens
like a tent-cloth;
    R:
You have constructed your palace
upon the waters.
You make the clouds your chariot;
you travel on the wings of the wind.
You make the winds your messengers,
and flaming fire your ministers.
    R:

How manifold are your works, O Lord!
In wisdom you have wrought them all—
the earth is full of your creatures;
the sea also, great and wide,
in which are schools without number
of living things both small and great.
    R:
They look to you to give them
food in due time.
When you give it to them,
they gather it;
when you open your hand,
they are filled with good things.
    R:
If you take away their breath
they perish and return to the dust.
When you send forth your spirit,
they are created, and you renew
the face of the earth.
    R:

SECOND READING

- Titus 2:11-14; 3: 4-7 -

Beloved: The grace of God has appeared, saving all and training us to reject godless ways and worldly desires and to live temperately, justly, devoutly in this age, as we await the blessed hope, the appearance of the glory of our great God and savior Jesus Christ, who gave himself for us to deliver us from all lawlessness and to cleanse for himself a people as his own, eager to do what is good.

When the kindness and generous love of God our savior appeared, not because of any righteous deeds we had done but because of his mercy, he saved us through the bath of rebirth and renewal by the Holy Spirit, whom he richly poured out on us through Jesus Christ our savior, so that we might be justified by his grace and become heirs in hope of eternal life.

GOSPEL

- Luke 3:15-16, 21-22 -

The people were filled with expectation, and all were asking in their hearts whether John be the Christ. John answered them all, saying, "I am baptizing you with water, but one mightier than I is coming. I am not worthy to loosen the thongs of his sandals. He will baptize you with the Holy Spirit and fire."

After all the people had been baptized and Jesus also had been baptized and was praying, heaven was opened and the Holy Spirit descended upon him in bodily form like a dove. And a voice came from heaven, "You are my beloved Son; with you I am well pleased."

Sunday

OPENING PRAYER

Breathe into me, Holy Spirit,
that my thoughts may all be holy.

Move in me, Holy Spirit,
that my work, too, may be holy.

Attract my heart, Holy Spirit,
that I may love only what is holy.

Strengthen me, Holy Spirit,
that I may defend all that is holy.

Protect me, Holy Spirit,
that I may always be holy. Amen.

—Prayer to the Holy Spirit by Saint Augustine

LECTIO DIVINA ✒ SACRED READING OF SCRIPTURE

Feel free to take notes on the video reflection in the space below.

LECTIO DIVINA ✒ MEDITATION

In the video, the presenter talks about three effects of baptism. What are these three changes?

Can you think of some ways other than those shared by the presenter in which we all still experience the consequences of Original Sin?

At baptism, the Holy Spirit descends upon us in order to help us to become more like Jesus. What are some of the ways that the Spirit aids us to be more Christ-like?

LECTIO DIVINA ☙ PRAYER & RESOLUTION

PRAYER: Prayerfully ponder how through the sacrament of baptism which you have received (or hope to receive soon), it is as if God the Father says the same thing to you as he said to Jesus: "You are my beloved son (or daughter); with you I am well pleased." Consider three key words in this statement: beloved, son and well pleased. What does it mean to you to know you are truly beloved by God; that you are a son (or daughter) of the heavenly Father; and that with you, God is well pleased?

RESOLUTION: This week, take time each day to consider how much God the Father loves you. If you find yourself becoming downhearted or critical, stop and repeat the words of the Gospel, using your own name; for example, "You (name) are my beloved son (or daughter); with you I am well pleased." Allow God's love to fill your heart and wash away your feelings of inadequacy or false guilt.

Monday

Write down the first images that come to mind when you think of God the Father, God the Son, and God the Holy Spirit. Reflect on how these images impact the way you pray.

> *"The First Person is called the Father and the Second the Son. We say that the First begets or produces the second; we call it begetting, not making, because what He produces is of the same kind as himself. In that way the word Father is the only word to use. But unfortunately it suggests that he is there first—just as a human father exists before his son... we must think of the Son always, so to speak, streaming forth from the Father, like light from a lamp, or heat from a fire, or thoughts from a mind. He is the self-expression of the father— what the father has to say. And there was never a time when he was not saying it."*
>
> —C.S. Lewis, *Mere Christianity*

Tuesday

In the first reading, we are told that the Lord feeds his flock like a shepherd and tends to the lambs and ewes. Reflect on ways that you have felt the Lord's care this week.

"The LORD is my shepherd;/ there is nothing I lack." —Psalm 23:1

Wednesday

Reread the Baptismal Promises from Sunday's prayer. Prayerfully and thoughtfully consider each statement and then write out your own set of promises of Faith.

"In Baptism every Christian personally meets him; he is inserted into the mystery of Christ's death and resurrection and receives a new life, which is the life of God. What a great gift and what a great responsibility!"

—Blessed Pope John Paul II (January 12, 2003).

Thursday

In the second reading, from Titus, we are told, "He saved us through the bath of rebirth and renewal by the Holy Spirit." What areas in your life need to be rebirthed and renewed by the Holy Spirit? List them and then ask the Spirit to come and guide you.

Come Holy Ghost, Creator Blest,
And in our hearts take up thy rest;
Come with thy grace and heav'nly aid
To fill the hearts which thou hast made,
To fill the hearts which thou hast made.

Friday

Even though Jesus was sinless, he still submitted to the baptism by John. How does his example of humility before the Father inspire you? How can you best emulate Jesus' example this week?

"We repeat with the New Testament, with the creed, and with Vatican Council II that Jesus Christ "has truly been made one of us, like us in all things except sin." It is precisely thanks to this likeness that "Christ, the final Adam, by the revelation of the mystery of the Father and his love, fully reveals man to man himself and makes his supreme calling clear."

—Blessed Pope John Paul II (February 3, 1988).

Saturday

The responsorial psalm says: "When you give it to them, they gather it." What gifts is God giving to you today? How can you gather in God's gifts? Be sure to remember to give thanks for all that the Lord provides.

"Every good gift and every perfect gift is from…the Father." —James 1:17 (RSV)

2ND SUNDAY IN ORDINARY TIME
❧ YEAR C ❧

DO WHATEVER HE TELLS YOU

READINGS FOR THE SECOND SUNDAY IN ORDINARY TIME

FIRST READING
- Isaiah 62:1-5 -

For Zion's sake I will not be silent,/ for Jerusalem's sake I will not be quiet,/ until her vindication shines forth like the dawn/ and her victory like a burning torch.

Nations shall behold your vindication,/ and all the kings your glory;/ you shall be called by a new name/ pronounced by the mouth of the Lord./ You shall be a glorious crown in the hand of the Lord,/ a royal diadem held by your God./ No more shall people call you "Forsaken,"/ or your land "Desolate,"/ but you shall be called "My Delight,"/ and your land "Espoused."/ For the Lord delights in you/ and makes your land his spouse./ As a young man marries a virgin,/ your Builder shall marry you;/ and as a bridegroom rejoices in his bride/ so shall your God rejoice in you.

RESPONSORIAL PSALM
- Psalm 96:1-2, 2-3, 7-8, 9-10 -

R: **Proclaim his marvelous deeds to all the nations.**

Sing to the Lord a new song;
sing to the Lord, all you lands.
Sing to the Lord; bless his name.
R:
Announce his salvation, day after day.
Tell his glory among the nations;
among all peoples, his wondrous deeds.
R:
Give to the Lord, you families of nations,
give to the Lord glory and praise;
give to the Lord the glory due his name!
R:
Worship the Lord in holy attire.
Tremble before him, all the earth;
say among the nations: the Lord is king.
He governs the peoples with equity.
R:

SECOND READING

~ 1 Corinthians 12:4-11 ~

Brothers and sisters: There are different kinds of spiritual gifts but the same Spirit; there are different forms of service but the same Lord; there are different workings but the same God who produces all of them in everyone. To each individual the manifestation of the Spirit is given for some benefit. To one is given through the Spirit the expression of wisdom; to another, the expression of knowledge according to the same Spirit; to another, faith by the same Spirit; to another, gifts of healing by the one Spirit; to another, mighty deeds; to another, prophecy; to another, discernment of spirits; to another, varieties of tongues; to another, interpretation of tongues. But one and the same Spirit produces all of these, distributing them individually to each person as he wishes.

GOSPEL

~ John 2:1-11 ~

There was a wedding at Cana in Galilee, and the mother of Jesus was there. Jesus and his disciples were also invited to the wedding. When the wine ran short, the mother of Jesus said to him, "They have no wine." And Jesus said to her, "Woman, how does your concern affect me? My hour has not yet come." His mother said to the servers, "Do whatever he tell you." Now there were six stone water jars there for Jewish ceremonial washings, each holding twenty to thirty gallons. Jesus told them, "Fill the jars with water." So they filled them to the brim. Then he told them, "Draw some out now and take it to the headwaiter." So they took it. And when the headwaiter tasted the water that had become wine, without knowing where it came from—although the servers who had drawn the water knew—the headwaiter called the bridegroom and said to him, "Everyone serves good wine first, and then when people have drunk freely, an inferior one; but you have kept the good wine until now." Jesus did this as the beginning of his signs at Cana in Galilee and so revealed his glory, and his disciples began to believe in him.

Sunday

OPENING PRAYER

O Mary, into your maternal hands I place myself and I abandon myself completely, sure of obtaining whatever I ask of you. I trust in you because you are the sweet Mother, I confide in you because you are the Mother of Jesus. In this trust I place myself, sure of being heard in everything; with this trust in my heart I greet you "my Mother, my trust," I devote myself entirely to you, begging you to remember that I am yours, that I belong to you; keep me and defend me, O sweet Mary, and in every instant of my life, present me to your Son, Jesus. Amen.

—St. Gianna Beretta Molla

LECTIO DIVINA ⤬ SACRED READING OF SCRIPTURE

Feel free to take notes on the video reflection in the space below.

LECTIO DIVINA ⤬ MEDITATION

Through the witness of the Blessed Mother and the servants, the wedding at Cana gives the reader some insight into what a disciple of Jesus is meant to look like. How do Mary's actions in this story provide a model for Christian discipleship?

How can you better follow her instruction to "do whatever he tells you"?

How does the response of the servants demonstrate the way of Christian discipleship?

How can it be a model in your own life?

LECTIO DIVINA ⸎ PRAYER & RESOLUTION

PRAYER: Imagine being at the wedding at Cana, witnessing Christ's miraculous action and the interaction of his Mother and the wedding servants. You become aware that Mary is speaking to Jesus and pointing to the empty wine jars. You see him go to the servants and give them an order. You watch in amazement as the servants begin to fill the jars with water and then, in complete astonishment, as they draw rich red wine from what was water. Now imagine Mary speaking the same words to you that she gave to the servants: "Do whatever he tells you." If Mary spoke these words directly to you today, to what one area in your life might the call to "do whatever he tells you" apply the most?

RESOLUTION: In your prayer this week, focus on this one specific area where you sense you are supposed to "do whatever he tells you" more obediently. Turn to Jesus and ask for guidance in this area of your life. Lovingly tell him you desire to serve him in this area with the same trusting obedience that Mary and the servants gave him at Cana.

"Christianity without discipleship is always Christianity without Christ."
—Dietrich Bonhoeffer

Monday

Reread the second reading from Paul's letter to the Corinthians where Paul talks about different spiritual gifts. As Christians, we believe that each one of us has received at least one spiritual gift at the time of our baptism and confirmation. As you pray this week, ask the Holy Spirit to show you what gifts you have been given and how you can use those gifts for the kingdom of God.

"Understanding is the reward of obedience. Obedience is the key to every door."

—George MacDonald

Tuesday

In the Gospel passage this week, we see Mary interceding on behalf of the wedding couple for their needs when the wine ran out (John 2:1-11). In our own lives, Mary is there to intercede for us and bring our needs to her Son. In what ways are you seeking out the guidance and intercession of our Blessed Mother? How could you turn to her on a more regular basis?

"We never give more honour to Jesus than when we honour his Mother, and we honour her simply and solely to honour him all the more perfectly. We go to her only as a way leading to the goal we seek—Jesus, her Son." —Saint Louis Marie de Montfort

Wednesday

In the first reading, Isaiah portrays a God who is intimately in love with his creation, modeling that love on the love between a husband and a wife (Isaiah 62:1-5). How does God show you this love on a daily basis? How can you be more open to receiving his love in your life?

"For if man exists it is because God has created him through love, and through love continues to hold him in existence."

—CCC 27

Thursday

Jesus chose a wedding to perform his first public miracle, demonstrating how much God delights in the Sacrament of Marriage. In prayer, thank God for the gift of marriage in your own life, whether it be your own or others you know who model God's design for marriage.

"Husbands, love your wives, even as Christ loved the Church and handed himself over for her."

—Ephesians 5:25

Friday

In the Gospel reading, the use of wine is central to the story (John 2:1-11). Wine represents the fullness and abundance of life that God desires us to have. In prayer today, praise God for how he provides abundantly for you in your life.

"Joy is the serious business of heaven."—C.S Lewis

Saturday

As you look over the Gospel passage one more time (John 2:1-11), pick out your favorite phrase or element of the story. Why does it speak to you?

"I would not believe the Gospels had not the authority of the Catholic Church already moved me."—St. Augustine

3RD SUNDAY
IN ORDINARY TIME
❧ YEAR C ❧

JUBILEE:
NEW
BEGINNINGS

READINGS FOR THE THIRD SUNDAY IN ORDINARY TIME

FIRST READING
- Nehemiah 8:2-4a, 5-6, 8-10 -

Ezra the priest brought the law before the assembly, which consisted of men, women, and those children old enough to understand. Standing at one end of the open place that was before the Water Gate, he read out of the book from daybreak till midday, in the presence of the men, the women, and those children old enough to understand; and all the people listened attentively to the book of the law. Ezra the scribe stood on a wooden platform that had been made for the occasion. He opened the scroll so that all people might see it—for he was standing higher up than any of the people—and, as he opened it, all the people rose. Ezra blessed the Lord, the great God, and all the people, their hands raised high, answered, "Amen, amen!" Then they bowed down and prostrated themselves before the Lord, their faces to the ground. Ezra read plainly from the book of the law of God, interpreting it so that all could understand what was read. Then Nehemiah, that is, His Excellency, and Ezra the priest-scribe and the Levites who were instructing the people said to all the people: "Today is holy to the Lord your God. Do not be sad, and do not weep"—for all the people were weeping as they heard the words of the law. He said further: "Go, eat rich foods and drink sweet drinks, and allot portions to those who had nothing prepared; for today is holy to our Lord. Do not be saddened this day, for rejoicing in the Lord must be your strength!

Responsorial Psalm
- Psalm 19:8, 9, 10, 15 -

R: **Your words, Lord, are Spirit and life.**

The law of the Lord is perfect,
refreshing the soul;
the decree of the Lord is trustworthy,
giving wisdom to the simple.
R:

The precepts of the Lord are right,
rejoicing the heart;
the command of the Lord is clear,
enlightening the eye.
R:

The fear of the Lord is pure,
enduring forever;
the ordinances of the Lord are true,
all of them just.
R:

Let the words of my mouth and the thought of my heart
find favor before you,
O Lord, my rock and my redeemer.
R:

Second Reading

- 1 Corinthians 12:12-30 -

Brothers and sisters: As a body is one though it has many parts, and all the parts of the body, though many, are one body, so also Christ. For in one Spirit we were all baptized into one body, whether Jews or Greeks, slaves or free persons, and we were all given to drink of one Spirit.

Now the body is not a single part, but many. If a foot should say, "Because I am not a hand I do not belong to the body," it does not for this reason belong less to the body. Or if an ear should say, "Because I am not an eye I do not belong to the body," it does not for this reason belong any less to the body. If the whole body were an eye, where would the hearing be? If the whole body were hearing, where would the sense of smell be? But as it is, there are many parts, yet one body. The eye cannot say to the hand, "I do not need you," nor again the head to the feet, "I do not need you." Indeed, the parts of the body that seem to be weaker are all the more necessary, and those parts of the body that we consider less honorable we surround with greater propriety, whereas our more presentable parts do not need this. But God has so constructed the body as to give greater honor to a part that is without it, so that there may be no division in the body, but that the parts may have the same concern for one another. If one part suffers, all the parts suffer with it; if one part is honored, all the parts share its joy.

Now you are Christ's body, and individually parts of it. Some people God has designated in the church to be, first, apostles; second, prophets; third, teachers; then, mighty deeds; then of healing, assistance, administration, and varieties of tongues. Are all apostles? Are all prophets? Are all teachers? Do all work mighty deeds? Do all have gifts of healing? Do all speak in tongues? Do all interpret?

GOSPEL

- Luke 1:1-4; 4:14-21 -

Since many have undertaken to compile a narrative of the events that have been fulfilled among us, just as those eyewitnesses from the beginning and ministers of the word have handed them down to us, I too have decided, after investigating everything accurately anew, to write it down in an orderly sequence for you, most excellent Theophilus, so that you may realize the certainty of the teachings you have received.

Jesus returned to Galilee in the power of the Spirit, and news of him spread throughout the whole region. He taught in their synagogues and was praised by all.

He came to Nazareth, where he had grown up, and went according to his custom into the synagogue on the Sabbath day. He stood up to read and was handed a scroll of the prophet Isaiah. He unrolled the scroll and found the passage where it was written: The Spirit of the Lord is upon me,/ because he has anointed me/ to bring glad tidings to the poor./ He has sent me to proclaim liberty to captives/ and recovery of sight to the blind,/ to let the oppressed go free,/ and to proclaim a year acceptable to the Lord./ Rolling up the scroll, he handed it back to the attendant and sat down, and the eyes of all in the synagogue looked intently at him. He said to them, "Today this Scripture passage is fulfilled in your hearing."

Sunday

OPENING PRAYER

Bless the LORD, my soul!
LORD, my God, you are great indeed!
You are clothed with majesty and glory,
robed in light as with a cloak.
You spread out the heavens like a tent;
you raised your palace upon the waters.
You make the clouds your chariot;
you travel on the wings of the wind.
You make the winds your messengers;
flaming fire, your ministers.
You fixed the earth on its foundation, never to be moved.

How varied are your works, LORD!
In wisdom you have wrought them all;
the earth is full of your creatures.
Look at the sea, great and wide!
It teems with countless beings,
living things both large and small.

All of these look to you
to give them food in due time.
When you give to them, they gather;
when you open your hand, they are well filled.
When you hide your face, they are lost.
When you take away their breath,
they perish and return to the dust from which they came.
When you send forth your breath, they are created,
and you renew the face of the earth.
May the glory of the LORD endure forever;
may the LORD be glad in these works!
—Psalm 104:1-5, 24-25, 27-31

O God, let your Spirit be upon us.
Let us hear your good news of release, sight, and liberty,
and rejoice together in your year of favor,
through Christ our Lord. Amen.

LECTIO DIVINA ✺ SACRED READING OF SCRIPTURE

Feel free to take notes on the video reflection in the space below.

LECTIO DIVINA ✺ MEDITATION

Why do you think that Jesus chose the passage from Isaiah that he did?

What was supposed to happen during the Jubilee Year?

How does the Jubilee apply to us?

All of us have certain spiritual blind spots, and we're often surprised when God opens our eyes to them. What is a spiritual blind spot and how can you make a new beginning once you recognize it?

Has there been a time in your life when someone paid a debt for you? Describe the gratitude you felt, and how you expressed it.

How can you express more gratitude to God for paying the debt of your sins on the cross?

LECTIO DIVINA ❧ PRAYER & RESOLUTION

PRAYER: Recall Jesus' words from today's Gospel reading about coming to proclaim liberty to the captives. Prayerfully ask Jesus to show you an area of your life where you are in slavery to sin and in need of the release, healing, and relief from oppression that he offers.

RESOLUTION: Recognizing our spiritual poverty—our complete dependence on God—talk to Jesus about areas where you need to be released and ask him what you can do to seek healing during the week. Ask for his help in this area.

"How beautiful upon the mountains/ are the feet of the one bringing good news,/ Announcing peace, bearing good news,/ announcing salvation, saying to Zion,/ 'Your God is King!' " —Isaiah 52:7

Monday

In the reading from Nehemiah 8, the people began weeping as they heard the Word of God read and explained to them. During prayer, recall a Scripture passage that strikes you with particular force, and reflect on what it means to you.

"For the word of God is living and active, sharper than any two-edged sword, piercing to the division of soul and spirit, of joints and marrow, and discerning the thoughts and intentions of the heart."—Hebrews 4:12 (RSV)

Tuesday

The reading this week from Nehemiah 8 advises the people not to grieve on hearing the word of God, but to celebrate a holy day, "for rejoicing in the Lord must be your strength." Do you experience joy as a feeling or as a decision? How does it strengthen you?

"Restore to me the joy of thy salvation, and uphold me with a willing spirit." —Psalm 51:12 (RSV)

Wednesday

In this week's Gospel reading, Luke states the reason why he wanted to write an "orderly sequence" for Theophilus (a name that means "friend of God"); namely, "that you may realize the certainty of the teachings you have received." Ask God to show you how knowing the truth can build your friendship with him.

"For with you is the fountain of life,/ and in your light we see light."

—Psalm 36:10

Thursday

The video this week compared the return of the land during the Jubilee year to the promise of Paradise that Jesus offered the "good thief" on the cross. How does that same promise affect the way you approach God?

"And he said to him, 'Truly, I say to you, today you will be with me in Paradise.'"

—Luke 23:43 (RSV)

Friday

Jesus' arrival in our midst means that we can be released from the slavery of sin. As you come before him in prayer this week, ask him to reveal to you an area of sin that enslaves you, one from which you have been unable to free yourself. Then write a short prayer for release from that sin.

"Blessed are those who wash their robes, that they may have the right to the tree of life." —Revelation 22:14 (RSV)

Saturday

When Jesus proclaims "a year acceptable to the Lord," his proclamation actually begins that "acceptable year." How has that "acceptable year" begun for you?

"He who has an ear, let him hear what the Spirit says to the churches. To him who conquers I will grant to eat of the tree of life, which is in the paradise of God." —Revelation 2:7 (RSV)

4TH SUNDAY
IN ORDINARY TIME
⚜ YEAR C ⚜

JESUS WAS SENT TO OUR ENEMIES, TOO

READINGS FOR THE FOURTH SUNDAY IN ORDINARY TIME

FIRST READING
- Jeremiah 1:4-5, 17-19 -

The word of the Lord came to me, saying:/ Before I formed you in the womb I knew you,/ before you were born I dedicated you,/ a prophet to the nations I appointed you.

But do you gird your loins;/ stand up and tell them/ all that I command you./ Be not crushed on their account,/ as though I would leave you crushed before them;/ for it is I this day/ who have made you a fortified city,/ a pillar of iron, a wall of brass,/ against the whole land:/ against Judah's kings and princes,/ against its priests and people./ They will fight against you but not prevail over you,/ for I am with you to deliver you, says the Lord.

RESPONSORIAL PSALM
- Psalm:71:1-6, 15, 17 -

R: **I will sing of your salvation.**

In you, O Lord, I take refuge;
let me never be put to shame.
In your justice rescue me, and deliver me;
incline your ear to me, and save me.
R:
Be my rock of refuge,
a stronghold to give me safety,
for you are my rock and my fortress.
O my God, rescue me from the hand of the wicked.
R:
For you are my hope, O Lord;
my trust, O God, from my youth.
On you I depend from birth;
from my mother's womb you are my strength.
R:
My mouth shall declare your justice,
day by day your salvation.
O God, you have taught me from my youth,
and till the present I proclaim your wondrous deeds.
R:

SECOND READING
~ 1 Corinthians 12:31–13:13 ~

Brothers and sisters: Strive eagerly for the greatest spiritual gifts. But I shall show you a still more excellent way.

If I speak in human and angelic tongues, but do not have love, I am a resounding gong or clashing cymbal. And if I have the gift of prophecy, and comprehend all mysteries and all knowledge; if I have all faith so as to move mountains, but do not have love, I am nothing. If I give away everything I own, and if I hand my body over so that I may boast, but do not have love, I gain nothing.

Love is patient, love is kind. It is not jealous, it is not pompous, it is not inflated, it is not rude, it does not seek its own interests, it is not quick-tempered, it does not brood over injury, it does not rejoice over wrongdoing but rejoices with the truth. It bears all things, believes all things, hopes all things, endures all things.

Love never fails. If there are prophecies, they will be brought to nothing; if tongues, they will cease; if knowledge, it will be brought to nothing. For we know partially and we prophesy partially, but when the perfect comes, the partial will pass away. When I was a child, I used to talk as a child, think as a child, reason as a child; when I became a man, I put aside childish things. At present we see indistinctly, as in mirror, but then face to face. At present I know partially; then I shall know fully, as I am fully known. So faith, hope, love remain, these three; but the greatest of these is love.

GOSPEL

- Luke 4:21-30 -

Jesus began speaking in the synagogue, saying: "Today this Scripture passage is fulfilled in your hearing." And all spoke highly of him and were amazed at the gracious words that came from his mouth. They also asked, "Isn't this the son of Joseph?" He said to them, "Surely you will quote me this proverb, 'Physician, cure yourself,' and say, 'Do here in your native place the things that we heard were done in Capernaum.'" And he said, "Amen, I say to you, no prophet is accepted in his own native place. Indeed, I tell you, there were many widows in Israel in the days of Elijah when the sky was closed for three and a half years and a severe famine spread over the entire land. It was to none of these that Elijah was sent, but only to a widow in Zarephath in the land of Sidon. Again, there were many lepers in Israel during the time of Elisha the prophet; yet not one of them was cleansed, but only Naaman the Syrian." When the people in the synagogue heard this, they were all filled with fury. They rose up, drove him out of the town, and led him to the brow of the hill on which their town had been built, to hurl him down headlong. But Jesus passed through the midst of them and went away.

Sunday

OPENING PRAYER

Lord, you call us to love our enemies and to pray for those who persecute us. We know we live in a dark world, where many people are opposed to the Gospel message and opposed to you. We pray today, that as we reflect on your Scriptures, we may be able to love our broken world as you do.

You call us to be the "light of the world." Lord, help us to shine your light in the darkest places. Help us to love as you love, and in doing so, win the world back to you.

We pray for the help and prayers of all the angels and saints as we pray these things through Jesus Christ our Lord. Amen.

LECTIO DIVINA ✒ SACRED READING OF SCRIPTURE

Feel free to take notes on the video reflection in the space below.

LECTIO DIVINA ✒ MEDITATION

One of the first places Jesus visits during the launch of his public ministry is his hometown of Nazareth. Why do you think Jesus decided to go there? And what might this tell us about how we are called to share our faith?

Who were considered the outsiders for the Jews in Jesus' day?

Who are the outsiders for us? What sorts of groups or people are we or our parish communities hesitant to extend mercy and welcome to?

It's sometimes hardest for us to share the Gospel with the people with whom we grew up: our own families and friends. Have you ever experienced this?

Why is it sometimes harder to share our faith with our parents, kids, spouses, siblings, than it is to share it with those who are less close to us?

LECTIO DIVINA ✺ PRAYER & RESOLUTION

PRAYER: Take some time to consider a person (or group of persons) that you struggle with, maybe someone who has hurt or insulted you. Now imagine that you were in the synagogue in Nazareth that day when Jesus came to teach. Envision Jesus telling everyone around you that he came to save the outsiders and the enemies of the people. Then imagine that Jesus singles you out from the crowd to tell you that he has even come to save that specific person who has hurt you. How would you feel if Jesus told you that? How would you respond to Jesus?

RESOLUTION: Take a few minutes to talk to Jesus about one or two practical ways that you can love that person who has been an enemy to you. This may be as simple as praying for that person or asking God to give you the grace to forgive a hurt from the past. Because all of our experiences are so different, ask God to show you what kind of love he wants you to give.

"We make our friends, we make our enemies; but God makes our next door neighbor." —G.K. Chesterton

Monday

The responsorial psalm from Sunday reads, "My mouth shall declare your justice, day by day your salvation." Sometimes God's salvation shows up in surprising places. In the Gospel reading, Luke 4:21-30, many of Jesus' contemporaries did not expect God's salvation to come to their enemies, but in reality, Jesus came to redeem the whole world—with no exceptions! In other words, Jesus has either redeemed the entire cosmos—or he hasn't! What does it mean to you that Jesus has come to save everything and everyone?

"What has not been assumed has not been healed."—St. Gregory Nazianzus

Tuesday

In Sunday's Gospel reading from Luke 4:21-30, Jesus returns to his hometown to begin sharing his saving message. His kinsmen become skeptical of the profound words coming from this man whom many of them had grown up with. Do you ever become skeptical of aspects of the Gospel message? In what ways do you fail to trust Jesus?

"Spread love everywhere you go: first of all in your own house. Give love to your children, to your wife or husband, to a next-door neighbor…Let no one ever come to you without leaving better and happier." —Blessed Teresa of Calcutta

Wednesday

In Sunday's second reading from the first letter of St. Paul to the Corinthians (12:31–13:13), the attributes of love are described. Reread 1 Corinthians 13:4-7. How can you apply these attributes of love to yourself?

"Oh, how great is the goodness of God, greater than we can understand. There are moments and there are mysteries of the divine mercy over which the heavens are astounded. Let our judgment of souls cease, for God's mercy upon them is extraordinary."

—CCC 2604

Thursday

In this Sunday's Gospel reading, many in the crowd listening to Jesus wanted God's wrath and punishment to fall on their enemies, while Jesus desired mercy and reconciliation for those same enemies. Which group—Jesus or the crowd—do you most closely associate with?

"So dearly does His Majesty love us that he will reward our love for our neighbor by increasing the love which we bear to himself, and that in a thousand ways." —St. Teresa of Avila

Friday

In Sunday's second reading from St. Paul's first letter to the Corinthians, he writes about putting aside "childish things." Elsewhere in the Gospels, Jesus encourages his followers to be "like little children." What do you think the difference is between "childishness" and being "child-like"?

"But Jesus said, 'Let the children come to me, and do not prevent them; for the kingdom of heaven belongs to such as these.'"—Matthew 19:14

Saturday

Read the Gospel account from Sunday, Luke 4:21-30. Imagine Jesus was someone you grew up with. Imagine he came to your parish to speak. Imagine he told your congregation that he wanted to reconcile your worst enemies. How would you respond?

"We can never have too much confidence in the good God who is so powerful and so merciful. We obtain from him as much as we hope for." —St. Theresa of Lisieux

5TH SUNDAY
IN ORDINARY TIME
❧ YEAR C ❧

ANSWERING THE CALL

READINGS FOR THE FIFTH SUNDAY IN ORDINARY TIME

FIRST READING
~ Isaiah 6:1-2a, 3-8 ~

In the year King Uzziah died, I saw the Lord seated on a high and lofty throne, with the train of his garment filling the temple. Seraphim were stationed above.

They cried one to the other, "Holy, holy, holy is the Lord of Hosts! All the earth is filled with his glory!" At the sound of that cry, the frame of the door shook and the house was filled with smoke.

Then I said, "Woe is me, I am doomed! For I am a man of unclean lips, living among a people of unclean lips; yet my eyes have seen the King, the Lord of hosts!" Then one of the seraphim flew to me, holding an ember that he had taken with tongs from the altar.

He touched my mouth with it, and said, "See, now that this has touched your lips, your wickedness is removed, your sin purged."

Then I heard the voice of the Lord saying, "Whom shall I send? Who will go for us?" "Here I am," I said; "send me!"

RESPONSORIAL PSALM
~ Psalm 138:1-2, 2-3, 4-5, 7-8 ~

R: **In the sight of the angels I will sing your praises, Lord.**

I will give thanks to you, O Lord, with all my heart,
for you have heard the words of my mouth;
in the presence of the angels I will sing your praise;
I will worship at your holy temple
and give thanks to your name.
R:

Because of your kindness and your truth;
for you have made great above all things
your name and your promise.
When I called, you answered me;
you built up strength within me.
R:

All the kings of the earth shall give thanks to you, O Lord,
when they hear the words of your mouth;
and they shall sing of the ways of the Lord:
"Great is the glory of the Lord."
R:

Your right hand saves me.
The Lord will complete what he has done for me;
your kindness, O Lord, endures forever;
forsake not the work of your hands.
R:

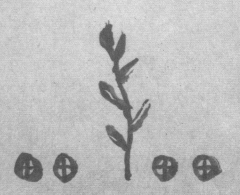

SECOND READING
- 1 Corinthians 15:1-11 -

I am reminding you, brothers and sisters, of the gospel I preached to you, which you indeed received and in which you also stand. Through it you are also being saved, if you hold fast to the word I preached to you, unless you believed in vain. For I handed on to you as of first importance what I also received: that Christ died for our sins in accordance with the Scriptures; that he was buried; that he was raised on the third day in accordance with the Scriptures; that he appeared to Cephas, then to the twelve. After that, he appeared to more than five hundred brothers at once, most of whom are still living, though some have fallen asleep. After that he appeared to James, then to all the apostles. Last of all, as to one born abnormally, he appeared to me. For I am the least of the apostles, not fit to be called an apostle, because I persecuted the church of God. But by the grace of God I am what I am, and his grace to me has not been ineffective. Indeed, I have toiled harder than all of them; not I, however, but the grace of God that is with me. Therefore, whether it be I or they, so we preach and so you believed.

OPTIONAL SHORT FORM

- 1 Corinthians 15:3-8, 11 -

Brothers and sisters, I handed on to you as of first importance what I also received: that Christ died for our sins in accordance with the Scriptures; that he was buried; that he was raised on the third day in accordance with the Scriptures; that he appeared to Cephas, then to the twelve. After that, he appeared to more than five hundred brothers at once, most of whom are still living, though some have fallen asleep. After that he appeared to James, then to all the apostles. Last of all, as to one abnormally born, he appeared to me. Therefore, whether it be I or they, so we preach and so you believed.

GOSPEL

- Luke 5:1-11 -

While the crowd was pressing in on Jesus and listening to the word of God, he was standing by the Lake of Gennesaret. He saw two boats there alongside the lake; the fishermen had disembarked and were washing their nets. Getting into one of the boats, the one belonging to Simon, he asked him to put out a short distance from the shore. Then he sat down and taught the crowds from the boat. After he had finished speaking, he said to Simon, "Put out into deep water and lower your nets for catch." Simon said in reply, "Master, we have worked hard all night and have caught nothing, but at your command I will lower the nets." When they had done this, they caught a great number of fish and their nets were tearing. They signaled to their partners in the other boat to come to help them. They came and filled both boats so that the boats were in danger of sinking. When Simon Peter saw this, he fell at the knees of Jesus and said, "Depart from me, Lord, for I am a sinful man." For astonishment at the catch of fish they had made seized him and all those with him, and likewise James and John, the sons of Zebedee, who were partners of Simon. Jesus said to Simon, "Do not be afraid; from now on you will be catching men." When they brought their boats to the shore, they left everything and followed him.

Sunday

OPENING PRAYER

Father, we're your people, the work of your hands.
So precious are we in your sight that you sent your Son, Jesus.
Jesus calls us to heal the broken-hearted,
to dry the tears of those who mourn, to give hope to those who despair,
and to rejoice in your steadfast love.
We, the baptized, realize our call to serve.
Help us to know how.
Call forth from among us priests, sisters, brothers, and lay ministers.
With our hearts you continue to love your people.
We ask this through our Lord Jesus Christ, your Son,
who lives and reigns with you and the Holy Spirit,
one God forever and ever. Amen.

LECTIO DIVINA ❧ SACRED READING OF SCRIPTURE

Feel free to take notes on the video reflection in the space below.

LECTIO DIVINA ❧ MEDITATION

How does Simon Peter respond to the miraculous catch of fish?

How does Jesus handle Simon's response?

Simon Peter felt unworthy to answer Jesus' call to discipleship. In what ways have you resisted God's call in the past (or present) because of feeling unworthy or unequipped?

LECTIO DIVINA ⁂ PRAYER & RESOLUTION

PRAYER: Prayerfully place yourself in today's Gospel reading. Imagine that you are with Simon Peter on his boat. You have just returned from an exhausting night of fishing without catching anything. But before you can go home and rest, Jesus gets into the boat and tells Peter to put out into the deep. You have heard Jesus' command, but you know that it is very unlikely you will catch any fish—what do you think about this command? Peter asks you to help cast the net. You do so and, against all odds, you pull in a miraculous catch of fish! How do you feel after you see this awesome miracle? What do you think of your previous disbelief? How might this make you approach your relationship with Jesus differently? What might you say to Peter? What might you say to Jesus?

RESOLUTION: Now imagine that after Jesus calls Simon Peter and tells him he will be catching men from now on, Jesus next turns to you. He tells you, "Follow me." In what particular way might Jesus be calling you to follow him more closely this week? Make a resolution that helps you to do that more this week, and ask Jesus for the grace to help you fulfill your resolution.

"He does not ask our worthiness; he asks our openness. I desire my life to be a source of hope for others, a sign that God wills to work out his unique designs in each one of us." —Blessed Teresa of Calcutta

Monday

In last Sunday's first reading, the prophet Isaiah confesses that he is "a man of unclean lips, living among a people of unclean lips" when he is confronted with the vision of the thrice-holy God. What sins of the lips have you committed—unkind words, gossip, failing to speak up when you should have? Take some time in prayer to ask God for forgiveness, and ask him how you can better dedicate your lips to his service.

"A fountain of life is the mouth of the just,/ but the mouth of the wicked conceals violence."—Proverbs 10:11

Tuesday

Last Sunday's responsorial psalm includes the verses: "I will give thanks to you, O LORD, with all my heart,/ for you have heard the words of my mouth;/ in the presence of the angels I will sing your praise;/ I will worship at your holy temple/ and give thanks to your name" (Psalm 138:1-2). We worship in the presence of the angels in a particular way at Mass. How can you act on this awareness and live out this psalm?

"Receiving the Eucharist means adoring him whom we receive. Only in this way do we become one with him, and are given, as it were, a foretaste of the beauty of the heavenly liturgy. The act of adoration outside Mass prolongs and intensifies all that takes place during the liturgical celebration itself."—Pope Benedict XVI

Wednesday

Reread last Sunday's second reading from 1 Corinthians 15:1-11. According to St. Paul, what are the key points of the Gospel he received and preached? How can you "hold fast" to these key points to keep from "believing in vain"?

"In giving us his Son, his only Word (for he possesses no other), he spoke everything to us at once in this sole Word—and he has no more to say… because what he spoke before to the prophets in parts, he has now spoken all at once by giving us the All who is his Son."

—St. John of the Cross

Thursday

Reread the Gospel reading from last Sunday: Luke 5:1-11. Reflect on St. Peter's response to Jesus, "Master, we have worked hard all night and have caught nothing, but at your command I will lower the nets." Peter is willing to obey Jesus' command, even though it doesn't make sense to him. How willing are you to obey God even when the reason or purpose of his command is not immediately obvious to you? What can you do to foster this spirit of obedience?

"The power of obedience! The lake of Gennesareth had denied its fishes to Peter's nets. A whole night in vain. Then, obedient, he lowered his net again to the water and they caught 'a huge number of fish.' Believe me: The miracle is repeated each day." —St. Josemaria Escriva

Friday

In last Sunday's second reading (1 Corinthians 15:1-11), St. Paul emphasizes that the Gospel message he has received and passed on is not his own, but something he received from those in authority, namely the apostles and Jesus himself. Reflect on the importance of the authority of the Gospel message. What do you do when this authority is challenged (either from outside or perhaps by your own doubts or questions)?

> *"What Christ entrusted to the apostles, they in turn handed on by their preaching and writing, under the inspiration of the Holy Spirit, to all generations, until Christ returns in glory."* —CCC 96

Saturday

Last Sunday's first reading ends with Isaiah answering God's call. God has a mission specifically for you—to what is he calling you? Are you ready to say "Here I am, send me"? Why or why not? Take some time in your prayer today to pray for discernment and courage to answer God's call.

> *"I will attempt day by day to break my will into pieces. I want to do God's holy will, not my own!"*—St. Gabriel of Our Lady of Sorrows

NOTE: Year C, 2013 and 2016 you will skip over to page 151 for the First Sunday of Lent.

6TH SUNDAY
IN ORDINARY TIME
❧ YEAR C ❧

THE SEARCH FOR TRUE HAPPINESS

READINGS FOR THE SIXTH SUNDAY IN ORDINARY TIME

FIRST READING
- Jeremiah 17:5-8 -

Thus says the LORD:/ Cursed is the one who trusts in human beings,/ who seeks his strength in flesh,/ whose heart turns away from the LORD./ He is like a barren bush in the desert/ that enjoys no change of season,/ but stands in a lava waste,/ a salt and empty earth./ Blessed is the one who trusts in the LORD,/ whose hope is the LORD./ He is like a tree planted beside the waters/ that stretches out its roots to the stream:/ it fears not the heat when it comes;/ its leaves stay green;/ in the year of drought it shows no distress,/ but still bears fruit.

RESPONSORIAL PSALM
- Psalm 1:1-2, 3, 4 and 6 -

R: **Blessed are they who hope in the Lord.**

Blessed the man who follows not
the counsel of the wicked,
nor walks in the way of sinners,
nor sits in the company of the insolent,
but delights in the law of the LORD
and meditates on his law day and night.
R:

He is like a tree
planted near running water,
that yields its fruit in due season,
and whose leaves never fade.
Whatever he does, prospers.
R:

Not so the wicked, not so;
they are like chaff which the wind drives away.
For the LORD watches over the way of the just,
but the way of the wicked vanishes.
R:

SECOND READING
- 1 Corinthians 15:12, 16-20 -

Brothers and sisters: If Christ is preached as raised from the dead, how can some among you say there is no resurrection of the dead? If the dead are not raised, neither has Christ been raised, and if Christ has not been raised, your faith is vain; you are still in your sins. Then those who have fallen asleep in Christ have perished. If for this life only we have hoped in Christ, we are the most pitiable people of all.

But now Christ has been raised from the dead, the first fruits of those who have fallen asleep.

GOSPEL
- Luke 6:17, 20-26 -

Jesus came down with the Twelve and stood on a stretch of level ground with a great crowd of his disciples and a large number of the people from all Judea and Jerusalem and the coastal region of Tyre and Sidon. And raising his eyes toward his disciples he said: "Blessed are you who are poor,/ for the kingdom of God is yours./ Blessed are you who are now hungry,/ for you will be satisfied./ Blessed are you who are now weeping,/ for you will laugh./ Blessed are you when people hate you,/ and when they exclude and insult you,/ and denounce your name as evil/l on account of the Son of Man./ Rejoice and leap for joy on that day!/ Behold, your reward will be great in heaven./ For their ancestors treated the prophets in the same way./ But woe to you who are rich,/ for you have received your consolation./ Woe to you who are filled now,/ for you will be hungry./ Woe to you who laugh now,/ for you will grieve and weep./ Woe to you when all speak well of you,/ for their ancestors treated the false prophets in this way."

Sunday

OPENING PRAYER

"The beatitude we are promised confronts us with decisive moral choices....It teaches us that true happiness is not found in riches or well-being, in human fame or power, or in any human achievement—however beneficial it may be—such as science, technology, and art, or indeed in any creature, but in God alone, the source of every good and of all love." —CCC 1723

Heavenly Father, we implore you to show us what true happiness is. We ask that you open our hearts and remove any desire for wealth, power, and praise that keeps us from pursuing the ways of the Gospel. We thank you for sending us your Son in humility and poverty, showing us a way of life far more beautiful than we could have imagined. We ask all of this through your Son, Jesus Christ, our Lord. Amen.

LECTIO DIVINA ❧ SACRED READING OF SCRIPTURE

Feel free to take notes on the video reflection in the space below.

LECTIO DIVINA ❧ MEDITATION

According to the presenter, how does Christ's view of happiness differ with the cultural perceptions of his time?

How does the Christian way differ with our own world's understanding of happiness?

Take a look at the list of things we created at the beginning of this session that people today think will make them happy. If Jesus were looking at our list, what do you think he would say about these ideals?

Which ones do you think he would say are truly top priorities for living a happy and fulfilling life?

Which ideals on our list (if any) might he say are not as urgent? What might Jesus add to our list?

LECTIO DIVINA 🕉 PRAYER & RESOLUTION

PRAYER: Imagine yourself sitting at the feet of Jesus when he gave the Beatitudes. Hear him say that the rich and satisfied will be unhappy. Hear him offer a path of true happiness through humble obedience and faith. Do you accept this humble path? Do you choose his roadmap of happiness over the need for wealth, worldly success, and human praise and acceptance? Now if Jesus were to approach you and ask you where you are putting your emphasis, what do you say to him?

RESOLUTION: Now in prayer, ask Jesus to show you an area of your life where you are too focused on or too attached to the fortunes, pleasures, and comforts offered by this world. Also ask him to show you ways you can change the desires of your heart to bring them more in line with the Beatitudes. Think of one small change you can make to your life this week that will help you place more of your heart's focus on the kingdom of God.

"God cannot give us a happiness and peace apart from himself, because it is not there. There is no such thing." —C.S. Lewis

Monday

Reread the first reading from the prophet Jeremiah (Jeremiah 17:5-8). As you read, reflect on whom you choose to trust in your daily life. Do you put your faith in God and his plans for you, or do you try to figure it out yourself or seek the counsel of the world?

"He that takes truth for his guide, and duty for his end, may safely trust to God's providence to lead him aright."—Blaise Pascal

Tuesday

In the Gospel passage for this week, Jesus proclaims his message by first address-ing his disciples (Luke 6:20-26). While the message is proclaimed for all of humanity, Jesus specifically entrusts his message to his closest followers. In doing so, he is showing them how they too are called to teach his message. How are you called to spread the message of Christ this week?

"He has not made us for naught; he has brought us thus far, in order to bring us further, in order to bring us on to the end. He will never leave us nor forsake us; so that we may boldly say 'The Lord is my helper; I will not fear what flesh can do unto me!'"—Psalm 51:12 (RSV)

Wednesday

Reread the second reading from St. Paul to the Corinthians (1 Corinthians 15:12, 16-20). Reflect on the power and goodness of Christ's Resurrection and how without it we would have no Christian faith.

"God will never, never, never let us down if we have faith and put our trust in him. He will always look after us. So we must cleave to Jesus. Our whole life must simply be woven into Jesus."—Blessed Teresa of Calcutta

Thursday

The second reading from St. Paul speaks of the "hope" that we find in Christ being raised from the dead (1 Corinthians 15:19). Pray that God will instill this endless hope in your daily life, and ask God to show you concrete ways to live out this hope each day.

"'For I know the plans I have for you' says the Lord, plans for welfare and not for evil, to give you a future and a hope."
—Jeremiah 29:11 (RSV) (RSV)

Friday

Reflect on a time in your life when you chose what was popular or easy over the humble way of Christ. What would you do differently now? How could the Beatitudes provide you with guidance for the next time you encounter such a situation?

"The purpose of your life is far greater than your own personal fulfillment, your peace of mind, or even your happiness...if you want to know why you were placed on this planet, you must begin with God. You were born by his purpose and for his purpose."

—Rick Warren,
The Purpose Driven Life

Saturday

As you look over this week's Gospel reading one more time, what is your favorite verse or which passage spoke most to you over the course of this week (Luke 6:17, 20-26)?

"Pray without ceasing."—1 Thessalonians 5:17

NOTE: **Year C, 2013 and 2016 you will skip over to page 151 for the First Sunday of Lent.**

7TH SUNDAY
IN ORDINARY TIME
❧ YEAR C ❧

AMAZING LOVE

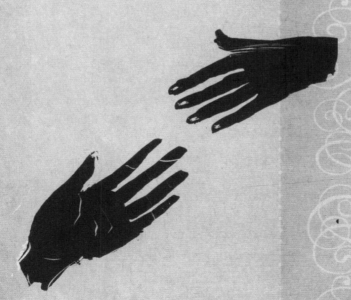

READINGS for the SEVENTH SUNDAY in ORDINARY TIME

FIRST READING
- 1 Samuel 26:2, 7-9, 12-13, 22-23 -

In those days, Saul went down to the desert of Ziph with three thousand picked men of Israel, to search for David in the desert of Ziph. So David and Abishai went among Saul's soldiers by night and found Saul lying asleep within the barricade, with his spear thrust into the ground at his head and Abner and his men sleeping around him.

Abishai whispered to David: "God has delivered your enemy into your grasp this day. Let me nail him to the ground with one thrust of the spear; I will not need a second thrust!" But David said to Abishai, "Do not harm him, for who can lay hands on the LORD's anointed and remain unpunished?" So David took the spear and the water jug from their place at Saul's head, and they got away without anyone's seeing or knowing or awakening. All remained asleep, because the LORD had put them into a deep slumber.

Going across to an opposite slope, David stood on a remote hilltop at a great distance from Abner, son of Ner, and the troops.

He said: "Here is the king's spear. Let an attendant come over to get it. The LORD will reward each man for his justice and faithfulness. Today, though the LORD delivered you into my grasp, I would not harm the LORD'S anointed."

RESPONSORIAL PSALM
- Psalm 103:1-4, 8, 10, 12-13 -

R: The Lord is kind and merciful.

Bless the LORD, O my soul;
and all my being, bless his holy name.
Bless the LORD, O my soul,
and forget not all his benefits.
R:

He pardons all your iniquities,
heals all your ills.
He redeems your life from destruction,
crowns you with kindness and compassion.
R:

Merciful and gracious is the LORD,
slow to anger and abounding in kindness.
Not according to our sins does he deal with us,
nor does he requite us according to our crimes.
R:

As far as the east is from the west,
so far has he put our transgressions from us.
As a father has compassion on his children,
so the LORD has compassion on those who fear him.
R:

SECOND READING
- 1 Corinthians 15:45-49 -

Brothers and sisters: It is written, The first man, Adam, became a living being, the last Adam a life-giving spirit. But the spiritual was not first; rather the natural and then the spiritual. The first man was from the earth, earthly; the second man, from heaven. As was the earthly one, so also are the earthly, and as is the heavenly one, so also are the heavenly. Just as we have borne the image of the earthly one, we shall also bear the image of the heavenly one.

GOSPEL
-Luke 6:27-38 -

Jesus said to his disciples: "To you who hear I say, love your enemies, do good to those who hate you, bless those who curse you, pray for those who mistreat you. To the person who strikes you on one cheek, offer the other one as well, and from the person who takes your cloak, do not withhold even your tunic. Give to everyone who asks of you, and from the one who takes what is yours do not demand it back. Do to others as you would have them do to you. For if you love those who love you, what credit is that to you? Even sinners love those who love them. And if you do good to those who do good to you, what credit is that to you? Even sinners do the same. If you lend money to those from whom you expect repayment, what credit is that to you? Even sinners lend to sinners, and get back the same amount. But rather, love your enemies and do good to them, and lend expecting nothing back; then your reward will be great and you will be children of the Most High, for he himself is kind to the ungrateful and the wicked. Be merciful, just as your Father is merciful.

"Stop judging and you will not be judged. Stop condemning and you will not be condemned. Forgive and you will be forgiven. Give, and gifts will be given to you; a good measure, packed together, shaken down, and overflowing, will be poured into your lap. For the measure with which you measure will in return be measured out to you."

Sunday

OPENING PRAYER

Lord, make me an instrument of your peace.
Where there is hatred, let me sow love;
where there is injury, pardon;
where there is doubt, faith;
where there is despair, hope;
where there is darkness, light;
and where there is sadness, joy.

O Divine Master, grant that I may not so much seek
to be consoled as to console;
to be understood as to understand;
to be loved as to love.
For it is in giving that we receive;
it is in pardoning that we are pardoned;
and it is in dying that we are born to eternal life.
Amen.

—Attributed to St. Francis of Assisi

LECTIO DIVINA 🕊 SACRED READING OF SCRIPTURE

Feel free to take notes on the video reflection in the space below.

LECTIO DIVINA 🕊 MEDITATION

Why do you think Jesus calls his followers to this kind of love?

How would you define the kind of love Jesus calls his disciples to, and how is this different from the way most of us understand love?

How can taking seriously this call in your daily life to love even your enemies make a difference in people's lives—whether it be the people you forgive or friends and family who witness your merciful response toward others who hurt you?

LECTIO DIVINA ❧ PRAYER & RESOLUTION

PRAYER: Take a moment now and close your eyes. Imagine that you are with the disciples as Jesus begins to talk. You hear him say, "To the person who strikes you on one cheek, offer the other one as well, and from the person who takes your cloak, do not withhold even your tunic. Give to everyone who asks of you, and from the one who takes what is yours do not demand it back. Do to others as you would have them do to you." What is your immediate reaction to hearing these things? In what ways is this teaching challenging for you?

RESOLUTION: Ask Jesus to show you one person who may have hurt you in the past but needs your love this week. What can you do to love this person, through thought, prayer, or even action? Pick one thing and resolve to do it as soon as possible this week.

"As a gift to humanity, which sometimes seems bewildered and overwhelmed by the power of evil, selfishness, and fear, the risen Lord offers his love that pardons, reconciles, and reopens hearts to love. It is love that converts hearts and gives peace. How much the world needs to understand and accept divine mercy!" —Blessed Pope John Paul II

Monday

Reread the responsorial psalm that was read this past Sunday (Psalm 103:1-4, 8, 10, 12-13). What word or phrase stands out to you? What does this reveal about God's mercy and forgiveness? Often in order to forgive as God forgives, we need to seek forgiveness for ourselves. In what ways do you need to seek forgiveness from God? from others?

> *"For Christ, while we were still helpless, yet died at the appointed time for the ungodly. Indeed, only with difficulty does one die for a just person, though perhaps for a good person one might even find courage to die. But God proves his love for us in that while we were still sinners Christ died for us."*
>
> —Romans 5:6-8

Tuesday

Before journaling today pray the Our Father, the prayer that Jesus himself taught us:

Our Father, who art in heaven,
Hallowed be thy name.
Thy kingdom come.
Thy will be done, on earth as it is in heaven.
Give us this day our daily bread.
And forgive us our trespasses,
as we forgive those who trespass against us.
And lead us not into temptation,
but deliver us from evil. Amen.

Then meditate for a few moments on the words "Forgive us our trespasses as we forgive those who trespass against us." These are daunting and challenging words—you are asking God to forgive you in the same way you forgive others. Here as in our Gospel reading for this week, Jesus again is calling you to love those who hurt and offend you.

How easily do you forgive others? Do you hold grudges or refuse to forgive? How can you become a more forgiving person?

"Now—and this is daunting—this outpouring of [God's] mercy cannot penetrate our hearts as long as we have not forgiven those who have trespassed against us."—CCC 2840

Wednesday

Read the first reading from last Sunday (1 Samuel 26:2; 7-9, 12-13, 22-23). Put yourself in the place of David who is confronted with his enemy's vulnerability.

What would you have done? Remember a time when you had a conflict or argument with someone. How did you react? In light of this reading and the Gospel reading this week, how would you handle it differently now?

"If a man finds it very hard to forgive injuries, let him look at a crucifix, and think that Christ shed all his blood for him, and not only forgave his enemies, but even prayed his heavenly Father to forgive them also."—St. Philip Neri

Thursday

Pray again the Peace Prayer attributed to St. Francis of Assisi with which we began the Sunday reflections:

Reflect on the day past. In what ways did I fail to emulate this Christ-like love? In what ways did I imitate this love? What can I do tomorrow to better love like Christ, especially those who are more difficult to love?

"For there are three ways of performing an act of mercy: the merciful word, by forgiving, and by comforting; secondly, if you can offer no word, then pray—that too is mercy; and thirdly, deeds of mercy. And when the Last Day comes, we shall be judged from this, and on this basis we shall receive the eternal verdict." —St. Faustina Kowalska

139

Friday

Reread Luke 6:33-36 from this week's Gospel reading:

Do you love others in a way that stands apart from everyone else? Do people see you as a child of the Most High by the way you live your life? How can you be a better witness of this love each day and with every person you encounter?

> **"This is my commandment:** *love one another as I love you. No one has greater love than this, to lay down one's life for one's friends."*
>
> —John 15:12-13

Saturday

Recall one specific passage from this week's readings that most touched you. Spend time responding to this passage in writing and prayer.

"Love is itself the fulfillment of all our works. There is one goal; that is why we run: We run toward it, and once we reach it, in it we shall find rest."

—St. Augustine

NOTE: **Year C, 2013 and 2016 you will skip over to page 151 for the First Sunday of Lent.**

8TH SUNDAY
IN ORDINARY TIME
❧ YEAR C ❧

BEARING
FRUIT

READINGS FOR THE EIGHTH SUNDAY IN ORDINARY TIME

FIRST READING
- Sirach 27:4-7 -

When a sieve is shaken, the husks appear;/ so do one's faults when one speaks./ As the test of what the potter molds is in the furnace,/ so tribulation is the test of the just./ The fruit of a tree shows the care it has had;/ so too does one's speech disclose the bent of one's mind./ Praise no one before he speaks,/ for it is then that people are tested.

RESPONSORIAL PSALM
- Psalm 92:2-3, 13-14, 15-16 -

R: **Lord, it is good to give thanks to you.**

It is good to give thanks to the LORD,
to sing praise to your name, Most High,
to proclaim your kindness at dawn
and your faithfulness throughout the night.
R:

The just one shall flourish like the palm tree,
like a cedar of Lebanon shall he grow.
They that are planted in the house of the LORD
shall flourish in the courts of our God.
R:

They shall bear fruit even in old age;
vigorous and sturdy shall they be,
declaring how just is the LORD,
my rock, in whom there is no wrong.
R:

SECOND READING
- 1 Corinthians 15:54-58 -

Brothers and sisters: When that which is corruptible clothes itself with incorruptibility,
then the word that is written shall come about: Death is swallowed up in victory./ Where, O death, is your victory?/ Where, O death, is your sting?/ The sting of death is sin, and the power of sin is the law. But thanks be to God who gives us the victory through our Lord Jesus Christ.

Therefore, my beloved brothers and sisters, be firm, steadfast, always fully devoted to the work of the Lord, knowing that in the Lord your labor is not in vain.

GOSPEL
- Luke 6:39-45 -

Jesus told his disciples a parable, "Can a blind person guide a blind person? Will not both fall into a pit? No disciple is superior to the teacher; but when fully trained, every disciple will be like his teacher. Why do you notice the splinter in your brother's eye, but do not perceive the wooden beam in your own? How can you say to your brother, 'Brother, let me remove that splinter in your eye,' when you do not even notice the wooden beam in your own eye? You hypocrite! Remove the wooden beam from your eye first; then you will see clearly to remove the splinter in your brother's eye.

"A good tree does not bear rotten fruit, nor does a rotten tree bear good fruit. For every tree is known by its own fruit. For people do not pick figs from thornbushes, nor do they gather grapes from brambles. A good person out of the store of goodness in his heart produces good, but an evil person out of a store of evil produces evil; for from the fullness of the heart the mouth speaks."

Sunday

OPENING PRAYER

Dear Jesus,
Help me to spread thy fragrance everywhere I go.
Flood my soul with thy spirit and love.
Penetrate and possess my whole being so utterly
that all my life may only be a radiance of thine.
Shine through me and be so in me
that every soul I come in contact with
may feel thy presence in my soul.
Let them look up and see no longer me but only Jesus.
Stay with me and then I shall begin to shine as you shine,
so to shine as to be a light to others. Amen.

—Blessed John Henry Newman

LECTIO DIVINA ✒ SACRED READING OF SCRIPTURE

Feel free to take notes on the video reflection in the space below.

LECTIO DIVINA ✒ MEDITATION

As we begin our reflection today, think about times in your life when you were facing great difficulties, trials, or hardships.

When you look back now, do you see ways in which you've grown through difficult times?

What positive "fruit" came out of those challenging moments in your life?

The verse from the second reading says, "Be firm, steadfast, always fully devoted to the work of the Lord, knowing that in the Lord, your labor is not in vain."

What is the "work" you think the Lord desires to do in your heart?

As we reflect on the readings today, what might be one particular "fruit" that the Lord desires to grow in your own life today?

What are some circumstances going on in your life right now that God might be using?

If you have been through a similar struggle in the past, can you share with the group how you grew through the trial?

LECTIO DIVINA   PRAYER & RESOLUTION

PRAYER: Imagine that you and Jesus are standing in today's Gospel reading under a fruit tree, loaded with ripening fruit. Jesus points to the fruit and says, "A good tree does not bear rotten fruit . . .every tree is known by its fruit." In prayer, ask Jesus to show you areas where you are not bearing good fruit—perhaps in your friendships or family life or in your moral life. If it's helpful, you could say the following prayer: "Lord, reveal to me the areas in my life where I am not bearing good fruit, where I am growing thorn bushes, or brambles, or even rotten fruit instead. I want to be the kind of person who sees my weaknesses, so that I can begin to seek your help to improve. Lord, help me see."

RESOLUTION: In prayer, discuss with Jesus one practical thing you can do this week to reduce the "bad fruit" in your life and increase the "good fruit."

"By your work you show what you love and what you know."
—St. Bruno

Monday

Reread the second reading from I Corinthians (I Corinthians 15:54-58). We reflected on this passage yesterday, and talked about the question "What is the "work" you think the Lord desires to do in your heart?" Take time today to stir up gratitude in your heart for that "work" of the Lord. How do you want to thank Jesus for that work that he is doing within you?

"I am confident of this, that the one who began a good work in you will continue to complete it until the day of Christ Jesus."—Philippians 1:6

Tuesday

This past Sunday we talked about the principal of growth—how we grow more from times of struggle and difficulty. Take time today to read the first reading again, Sirach 27:4-7. How do these verses speak to this spiritual principle?

"Remain in me, as I remain in you. Just as a branch cannot bear fruit on its own unless it remains on the vine, so neither can you unless you remain in me. I am the vine, you are the branches. Whoever remains in me and I in him will bear much fruit, because without me you can do nothing." —John 15:4-5

Wednesday

Reread the first verses of the responsorial psalm, Psalm 92:2-3. You have reflected the past couple of days on the work the Lord has done in your life, so take time today to be grateful, to give thanks.

"O give thanks to the Lord, call on his name; make known his deeds among the peoples!"—St. Philip Neri

Thursday

Reread Luke 6:41-42 where Jesus talks about taking the beam out of our own eye before being critical of the splinter in our neighbor's eye. Take a few minutes today to examine your life. Ask Jesus to help reveal any hidden sins or faults that you might not be recognizing.

"And it is the Lord, it is Jesus, who is my judge. Therefore I will try always to think leniently of others, that he may judge me leniently, or rather not at all, since he says: 'Judge not, and ye shall not be judged.'"
—St. Faustina Kowalska

149

Friday

Read Psalm 92:13-16 today. This is the second half of the responsorial psalm from this past Sunday. Reflect on the words and let them really sink in—meditate on them. How is the Lord speaking to you through these verses?

"If we truly think of Christ as our source of holiness, we shall refrain from anything wicked or impure in thought or act and thus show ourselves to be worthy bearers of his name. For the quality of holiness is shown not by what we say but by what we do in life."
—St. Gregory of Nyssa

Saturday

Reread the Gospel passage Luke 6:39-45. The other day, you imagined that you were one of the disciples with Jesus when he was giving this homily. Engage your imagination around this scene again as you read these words. What stands out to you today as you read this passage? How is the Lord inviting you to be his disciple?

"If you remain in me and my words remain in you, ask for whatever you want and it will be done for you. By this is my Father glorified, that you bear much fruit and become my disciples. As the Father loves me, so I also love you. Remain in my love." —John 15:7-9

1ST SUNDAY OF LENT
❧ YEAR C ❧

RESISTING TEMPTATION

READINGS for the FIRST SUNDAY of LENT

FIRST READING
- Deuteronomy 26:4-10 -

Moses spoke to the people, saying: "The priest shall receive the basket from you and shall set it in front of the altar of the LORD, your God. Then you shall declare before the LORD, your God, 'My father was a wandering Aramean who went down to Egypt with a small household and lived there as an alien. But there he became a nation great, strong, and numerous. When the Egyptians maltreated and oppressed us, imposing hard labor upon us, we cried to the LORD, the God of our fathers, and he heard our cry and saw our affliction, our toil, and our oppression. He brought us out of Egypt with his strong hand and outstretched arm, with terrifying power, with signs and wonders; and bringing us into this country, he gave us this land flowing with milk and honey. Therefore I have now brought you the first fruits of the products of the soil which you, O LORD, have given me.' And having set them before the LORD, your God, you shall bow down in his presence."

RESPONSORIAL PSALM
~ Psalm 91:1-2, 10-11, 12-13, 14-15 ~

R: **Be with me, Lord, when I am in trouble.**

You who dwell in the shelter of the Most High,
who abide in the shadow of the Almighty,
say to the LORD, "My refuge and fortress,
My God in whom I trust."
R:

No evil shall befall you,
nor shall affliction come near your tent,
for to his angels he has given command about you,
that they guard you in all your ways.
R:

Upon their hands they shall bear you up,
lest you dash your foot against a stone.
You shall tread upon the asp and the viper;
you shall trample down the lion and the dragon.
R:

Because he clings to me, I will deliver him;
I will set him on high because he acknowledges my name.
He shall call upon me, and I will answer him;
I will be with him in distress;
I will deliver him and glorify him.
R:

SECOND READING
~ Romans 10:8-13 ~

Brothers and sisters: What does Scripture say? The word is near you,/ in your mouth and in your heart/ —that is, the word of faith that we preach—for, if you confess with your mouth that Jesus is Lord and believe in your heart that God raised him from the dead, you will be saved. For one believes with the heart and so is justified, and one confesses with the mouth and so is saved. For the Scripture says No one who believes in him will be put to shame. For there is no distinction between Jew and Greek; the same Lord is Lord of all, enriching all who call upon him. For "everyone who calls on the name of the Lord will be saved."

GOSPEL

- Luke 4:1-13 -

Filled with the Holy Spirit, Jesus returned from the Jordan and was led by the Spirit into the desert for forty days, to be tempted by the devil. He ate nothing during those days, and when they were over he was hungry. The devil said to him, "If you are the Son of God, command this stone to become bread." Jesus answered him, "It is written, One does not live on bread alone." Then he took him up and showed him all the kingdoms of the world in a single instant. The devil said to him, "I shall give to you all this power and glory; for it has been handed over to me, and I may give it to whomever I wish. All this will be yours if you worship me." Jesus said to him in reply, "It is written: You shall worship the Lord, your God, and him alone shall you serve." Then he led him to Jerusalem, made him stand on the parapet of the temple, and said to him, "If you are the Son of God, throw yourself down from here, for it is written: He will command his angels concerning you, to guard you, and: With their hands they will support you, lest you dash your foot against a stone." Jesus said to him in reply, "It also says, You shall not put the Lord, your God, to the test." When the devil had finished every temptation, he departed from him for a time.

Sunday

OPENING PRAYER

Hear my words, O Lord; listen to my sighing.
Hear my cry for help, my king, my God!
To you I pray, O Lord; at dawn you will hear my cry;
at dawn I will pleased before you and wait.

You are not a god who delights in evil;
no wicked person finds refuge with you;
the arrogant cannot stand before you.
You hate all who do evil...

But I can enter your house because of your great love.
I can worship in your holy temple
because of my reverence for you, Lord.
Guide me in your justice because of my foes;
make straight your way before me. Amen.

—Psalm 5:1-6, 8-9

LECTIO DIVINA ❧ SACRED READING OF SCRIPTURE

Feel free to take notes on the video reflection in the space below.

LECTIO DIVINA ❧ MEDITATION

In what three ways did Satan tempt Jesus, and how does Satan use these same tactics to tempt us today?

Jesus responded to temptation using the Word of God. How are the Scriptures an important weapon and defense in our battle against temptation?

LECTIO DIVINA PRAYER & RESOLUTION

PRAYER: Prayerfully put yourself in today's Gospel reading. Imagine that you are present in the desert; you witness Satan tempting Jesus and Jesus faithfully resisting each of the three temptations. Next imagine that each temptation is presented directly to you. The devil tells you that (1) you are not really a child of God; (2) you can have anything you want in the world by turning away from God, and (3) you don't have to follow God's plan for your life but can choose an easier way instead. How would you respond to each of these temptations?

RESOLUTION: Prayerfully consider which of these temptations is most difficult for you to resist. Why is it? What can you do this week to resist this temptation more in your life?

"This is why Christ vanquished the Tempter for us: 'For we have not a high priest who is unable to sympathize with our weaknesses, but one who in every respect has been tested as we are, yet without sinning' (Hebrews 4:15). By the solemn forty days of Lent the Church unites herself each year to the mystery of Jesus in the desert." —CCC, 540

Monday

Reread last Sunday's first reading from Deuteronomy 26:4-10. This passage is a summary of Israel's identity—a chosen nation, ransomed by God. How does this passage help you be more secure and confident in your identity—a child of God, chosen and ransomed?

"It is better to be the child of God than king of the whole world."
—St. Aloysius Gonzaga

Tuesday

In last Sunday's Gospel reading we hear Jesus quoting Deuteronomy 6:16: "You shall not put the Lord, your God, to the test" (Luke 4:12). In what ways have you tested God in the past? In your prayer time today, ask for the grace to be humble and obedient rather than putting God to the test in the future.

"By obeying we raise ourselves beyond our littleness and we can act in conformity with an infinite wisdom....Through obedience we become infinitely powerful." —St. Maximilian Kolbe

Wednesday

In last Sunday's second reading, St. Paul quotes Deuteronomy 30:14 saying, "'The word is near you, in your mouth and in your heart'—that is, the word of faith that we preach" (Romans 10:8). What can you do this week to consciously keep the Word of God in your mouth and in your heart?

"Lent stimulates us to let the Word of God penetrate our life and in this way to know the fundamental truth: who we are, where we come from, where we must go, what path we must take in life."—Pope Benedict XVI

Thursday

In last Sunday's first reading from Deuteronomy 26:4-10, we read about how the Israelites were commanded to bring their first fruits before God. How can you offer God your "first fruits" this week?

"Honor the Lord with your wealth, with first fruits of all your produce; then will your barns be filled with grain, with new wine your vats will overflow."
—Proverbs 3:9-10

159

Friday

Last Sunday's second reading from Romans 10:8-13 reminds us that faith is a matter both for private conviction and public profession and action: "For one believes with the heart and so is justified, and one confesses with the mouth and so is saved" (Romans 10:10). Are you both believing in your heart and confessing with your mouth? What can you do to improve in either or both areas?

> *"Not everyone who says to me, 'Lord, Lord,' will enter the kingdom of heaven, but only the one who does the will of my Father in heaven."*
>
> —Matthew 7:21

Saturday

The responsorial psalm from last Sunday tells us, "for to his angels he has given command about you, that they guard you in all your ways" (Psalm 91:11). When have you experienced the protection of your guardian angel? How can you be more aware of this constant guard over you?

> *"When tempted, invoke your Angel. He is more eager to help you than you are to be helped! Ignore the devil and do not be afraid of him; he trembles and flees at the sight of your Guardian Angel."*
>
> —St. John Bosco

2ND SUNDAY OF LENT
✤ YEAR C ✤

LONGING FOR GLORY

READINGS FOR THE SECOND SUNDAY OF LENT

FIRST READING
- Genesis 15:5-12, 17-18 -

The Lord God took Abram outside and said, "Look up at the sky and count the stars, if you can. Just so," he added, "shall your descendants be." Abram put his faith in the LORD, who credited it to him as an act of righteousness.

He then said to him, "I am the LORD who brought you from Ur of the Chaldeans to give you this land as a possession." "O Lord God," he asked, "how am I to know that I shall possess it?" He answered him, "Bring me a three-year-old heifer, a three-year-old she-goat, a three-year-old ram, a turtledove, and a young pigeon." Abram brought him all these, split them in two, and placed each half opposite the other; but the birds he did not cut up. Birds of prey swooped down on the carcasses, but Abram stayed with them. As the sun was about to set, a trance fell upon Abram, and a deep, terrifying darkness enveloped him.

When the sun had set and it was dark, there appeared a smoking fire pot and a flaming torch, which passed between those pieces. It was on that occasion that the LORD made a covenant with Abram, saying: "To your descendants I give this land, from the Wadi of Egypt to the Great River, the Euphrates."

RESPONSORIAL PSALM
- Psalm 27:1, 7-8, 8-9, 13-14 -

R: **The Lord is my light and my salvation.**

The LORD is my light and my salvation;
Whom should I fear?
The LORD is my life's refuge;
of whom should I be afraid?
R:

Hear, O LORD, the sound of my call;
have pity on me, and answer me.
Of you my heart speaks; you my glance seeks.
R:

Your presence, O LORD, I seek.
Hide not your face from me;
do not in anger repel your servant.
You are my helper: cast me not off.
R:

I believe that I shall see the bounty of the LORD
in the land of the living.
Wait for the LORD with courage;
be stouthearted, and wait for the LORD.
R:

SECOND READING
- Philippians 3:17–4:1 -

[Shorter Form is indented in brackets]

Join with others in being imitators of me, brothers and sisters, and observe those who thus conduct themselves according to the model you have in us. For many, as I have often told you, and now tell you even in tears, conduct themselves as enemies of the cross of Christ. Their end is destruction. Their God is their stomach; their glory is in their "shame." Their minds are occupied with earthly things.

[But our citizenship is in heaven, and from it we also await a savior, the Lord Jesus Christ. He will change our lowly body to conform with his glorified body by the power that enables him also to bring all things into subjection to himself.

Therefore, my brothers and sisters, whom I love and long for, my joy and crown, in this way stand firm in the Lord.]

GOSPEL
- Luke 9:28b-36-

Jesus took Peter, John, and James and went up the mountain to pray. While he was praying his face changed in appearance and his clothing became dazzling white. And behold, two men were conversing with him, Moses and Elijah, who appeared in glory and spoke of his exodus that he was going to accomplish in Jerusalem. Peter and his companions had been overcome by sleep, but becoming fully awake, they saw his glory and the two men standing with him. As they were about to part from him, Peter said to Jesus, "Master, it is good that we are here; let us make three tents, one for you, one for Moses, and one for Elijah." But he did not know what he was saying. While he was still speaking, a cloud came and cast a shadow over them, and they became frightened when they entered the cloud. Then from the cloud came a voice that said, "This is my chosen Son; listen to him." After the voice had spoken, Jesus was found alone. They fell silent and did not at that time tell anyone what they had seen.

Sunday

OPENING PRAYER

"O God, thou art my God,
I seek thee,
my soul thirsts for thee;
my flesh faints for thee,
as in a dry and weary land
where no water is.
So I have looked upon thee in the sanctuary,
beholding thy power and glory.
Because thy steadfast love is better than life,
my lips will praise thee."—Psalm 63:1-3 (RSV)

Father, you revealed your chosen Son to his disciples,
giving them a glimpse of that glory which he had with you
from the beginning,
a foretaste of the glory he was to bring about
by the exodus he would accomplish in Jerusalem.
As we reflect on your Word,
open our hearts to an ardent longing for that same glory
promised to us who seek your face day after day.
Through Jesus Christ our Lord. Amen.

LECTIO DIVINA ❧ SACRED READING OF SCRIPTURE

Feel free to take notes on the video reflection in the space below.

LECTIO DIVINA ❧ MEDITATION

In the Gospel reading for this week, we are told that Jesus took Peter, John, and James with him up Mount Tabor to pray.

Why do you think Jesus took these three with him this time when he often went out alone to pray?

The Gospel passage makes it clear that the Transfiguration took place within the context of prayer: "While he was praying his face changed in appearance and his clothing became dazzling white." Jesus' appearance was changed while he was praying.

What kind of changes have you experienced in your life as a result of prayer—either while you have been praying or after you started to cultivate a habit of prayer?

LECTIO DIVINA ❧ PRAYER & RESOLUTION

PRAYER: **Prayerfully place yourself in today's Gospel reading. Imagine being one of the three apostles who had been chosen to ascend Mount Tabor with Jesus. If you had been one of the apostles, you would have seen Jesus practically every day for about three years following him in his public ministry. But now, you see Jesus like never before—transfigured and radiant in glory. Suddenly, in the midst of this extraordinary revelation of Jesus, a voice from heaven speaks. It is God the Father, saying "This is my Son, my Chosen; listen to him" (RSV). The one command the heavenly Father gives you in this most amazing moment of divine revelation is to listen to Jesus, his Son. Take time now in prayer to consider what ways Jesus may want you to listen to him more in your life.**

RESOLUTION: **Responding to the Father's command to "listen" to Jesus, come up with one specific resolution you can make this week to help you listen more closely to Jesus.**

"And the Word became flesh and made his dwelling among us, and we saw his glory, the glory as of the Father's only Son, full of grace and truth." —John 1:14

Monday

In yesterday's Gospel reading we heard God commanding us, "This is my chosen Son, listen to him" (Luke 9:35). How can you listen more attentively to Jesus this week?

"Listen carefully my son, to the master's instructions and attend to them with the ear of your heart." —St. Benedict

Tuesday

In Sunday's first reading from Genesis, God tells Abram that it was he who "brought you from Ur of the Chaldeans to give you this land as a possession" (Genesis 15:7). God is stating here both his promise and his purpose for Abram. Ultimately, God's promise and his purpose for you are the same — life with himself. As you pray, ask God to clarify how he wants you to attain both ends, and to reflect that in your conduct this week.

"You yourself encourage [man] to delight in your praise, for you have made us for yourself, and our heart is restless until it rests in you."
—St. Augustine, Confessions

Wednesday

In Sunday's first reading from Genesis, God invites Abram to "look up at the sky and count the stars, if you can. Just so, shall your descendants be." Even though it would be more than twenty years before Abram realized the beginning of that promise in the birth of Isaac, Abram "put his faith in the Lord" (Genesis 15:5-6). In your journal, identify an area of your life where your trust in God is weak, and ask him to help you trust him for that area.

"Let nothing trouble you, let nothing frighten you. Everything passes. God never changes. Patience obtains all. Whoever has God wants for nothing. God alone is enough." —St. Teresa of Avila

Thursday

The responsorial psalm for Sunday's readings contains this exhortation: "Of you my heart speaks; you my glance seeks. Your presence, O LORD, I seek! Hide not your face from me" (Psalm 27:8-9). During your prayer time, ask God to show you how to "seek his face" in your immediate circumstances, even those that are difficult.

"By prayer we can discern 'what is the will of God' and obtain the endurance to do it. Jesus teaches us that one enters the kingdom of heaven not by speaking words, but by doing 'the will of my Father in heaven.'"
—CCC 2826

169

Friday

In the second reading from last Sunday, St. Paul contrasts people whose "God is their stomach," whose "glory is in their 'shame,'" and whose "minds are occupied with earthly things" with people whose "citizenship is in heaven" (Philippians 3:19-20). Ask God to show you which side of this contrast occupies most of your thoughts, and pray for a greater desire for heaven.

> *"The desire for God is written in the human heart, because man is created by God and for God; and God never ceases to draw man to himself. Only in God will he find the truth and happiness he never stops searching for."*
>
> —CCC 27

Saturday

In last Sunday's second reading from Philippians, St. Paul urges us to "join with others in being imitators of me, brothers and sisters, and observe those who thus conduct themselves according to the model you have in us" (Philippians 3:17). Who in your life has been a particular model of what it means to conduct ourselves as St. Paul urges, remembering that "our citizenship is in heaven" (Philippians 3:20)? Take some time in prayer to reflect on their example and thank God for them.

> *"Remember your leaders who spoke the word of God to you. Consider the outcome of their way of life and imitate their faith."*
>
> —Hebrews 13:7

3RD SUNDAY OF LENT
❧ YEAR C ❧

TO WHOM MUCH IS GIVEN

READINGS FOR THE THIRD SUNDAY OF LENT

FIRST READING
- Exodus 3:1-8a, 13-15 -

Moses was tending the flock of his father-in-law Jethro, the priest of Midian. Leading the flock across the desert, he came to Horeb, the mountain of God. There an angel of the Lord appeared to Moses in fire flaming out of a bush. As he looked on, he was surprised to see that the bush, though on fire, was not consumed. So Moses decided, "I must go over to look at this remarkable sight and see why the bush is not burned."

When the Lord saw him coming over to look at it more closely, God called out to him from the bush, "Moses! Moses!" He answered, "Here I am." God said, "Come no nearer! Remove the sandals from your feet, for the place where you stand is holy ground. I am the God of your fathers," he continued, "the God of Abraham, the God of Isaac, the God of Jacob." Moses hid his face, for he was afraid to look at God. But the Lord said, "I have witnessed the affliction of my people in Egypt and have heard their cry of complaint against their slave drivers, so I know well what they are suffering. Therefore I have come down to rescue them from the hands of the Egyptians and lead them out of that land into a good and spacious land, a land flowing with milk and honey."

Moses said to God, "But when I go to the Israelites and say to them, 'The God of your fathers has sent me to you,' if they ask me, 'What is his name?' what shall I tell them?" God replied, "I am who am." Then he added, "This is what you shall tell the Israelites: I AM sent me to you."

God spoke further to Moses, "Thus shall you say to the Israelites: The Lord, the God of your fathers, the God of Abraham, the God of Isaac, the God of Jacob, has sent me to you. "This is my name forever; thus am I to be remembered through all generations.

RESPONSORIAL PSALM
~ Psalm 103:1-2, 3-4, 6-7, 8, 11 ~

R: **The Lord is kind and merciful.**

Bless the Lord, O my soul;
and all my being, bless his holy name.
Bless the Lord, O my soul,
and forget not all his benefits.
R:

He pardons all your iniquities,
heals all your ills.
He redeems your life from destruction,
crowns you with kindness and compassion.
R:

The Lord secures justice
and the rights of all the oppressed.
He has made known his ways to Moses,
and his deeds to the children of Israel.
R:

Merciful and gracious is the Lord,
slow to anger and abounding in kindness.
For as the heavens are high above the earth,
so surpassing is his kindness toward those who fear him.
R:

SECOND READING
~ 1 Corinthians 10:1-6, 10-12 ~

I do not want you to be unaware, brothers and sisters, that our ancestors were all under the cloud and all passed through the sea, and all of them were baptized into Moses in the cloud and in the sea. All ate the same spiritual food, and all drank the same spiritual drink, for they drank from a spiritual rock that followed them, and the rock was the Christ. Yet God was not pleased with most of them, for they were struck down in the desert. These things happened as examples for us, so that we might not desire evil things, as they did.

Do not grumble as some of them did, and suffered death by the destroyer. These things happened to them as an example, and they have been written down as a warning to us, upon whom the end of the ages has come. Therefore, whoever thinks he is standing secure should take care not to fall.

GOSPEL
- Luke 13:1-9 -

Some people told Jesus about the Galileans whose blood Pilate had mingled with the blood of their sacrifices. Jesus said to them in reply, "Do you think that because these Galileans suffered in this way they were greater sinners than all other Galileans? By no means! But I tell you, if you do not repent, you will all perish as they did! Or those eighteen people who were killed when the tower at Siloam fell on them—do you think they were more guilty than everyone else who lived in Jerusalem? By no means! But I tell you, if you do not repent, you will all perish as they did!"

And he told them this parable: "There once was a person who had a fig tree planted in his orchard, and when he came in search of fruit on it but found none, he said to the gardener, 'For three years now I have come in search of fruit on this fig tree but have found none. So cut it down. Why should it exhaust the soil?' He said to him in reply, 'Sir, leave it for this year also, and I shall cultivate the ground around it and fertilize it; it may bear fruit in the future. If not you can cut it down.'"

Sunday

OPENING PRAYER

Liberating God,
in love you have set us free:
free from slavery to sin and self,
free to know and love you,
free to follow and serve you.

We praise you for your faithful love toward us,
and for the many ways you have demonstrated
that love to us.
We see your love in the natural world around us—
in the sky and trees and rivers.
We see your love in the gift of
your commandments—
the rules for living that guide us into right
relationship with you,
and with the people around us.
And we see your love in Jesus Christ,
who lived and died to bring us life.

Because we have experienced your love,
we come before you with confidence,
bringing our needs and the needs of our world.
God, in your unfailing love, hear our prayer. Amen.

—Adapted from http://re-worship.blogspot.com/2011/09/prayers-of-people-october-2-2011.html

LECTIO DIVINA ❧ SACRED READING OF SCRIPTURE

Feel free to take notes on the video reflection in the space below.

LECTIO DIVINA ❧ MEDITATION

In the second reading, St. Paul tells his readers that all of the Exodus generation saw the mighty works of God, but that most of the Exodus generation fell away. What was the reason for this?

What lesson might we take away from this?

**Why did some of the Exodus generation want to go back to Egypt
even after they had been set free?**

Have you ever wanted to return to an old way of life that you had already left behind?

LECTIO DIVINA · PRAYER & RESOLUTION

PRAYER: Put yourself in today's Gospel reading and imagine that you hear Jesus talking about the fig tree that didn't bear fruit but was allowed to live another year. Imagine that he is saying those words to you. If you were given one more year to bear fruit, what sorts of things would you do?

RESOLUTION: In what areas of your spiritual or moral life have you found yourself tempted to be like Israel and want to "turn back"? What can you do to persevere so that you can bear more fruit in your life? Ask Jesus to show you where you need to make changes in your life in order to become a fruitful fig tree.

"The more one does what is good, the freer one becomes. There is no true freedom except in the service of what is good and just. The choice to disobey and do evil is an abuse of freedom and leads to 'the slavery of sin.'" —CCC 1733

Monday

This Sunday's readings all have to do with the Old Testament Exodus story, in which God freed his chosen people from their captivity in Egypt. What things enslave you in your everyday life? Your job? Relationships? Financial debt? What are some ways you can surrender these things to God and allow him to set you free?

"This is how Israel understands its liberation from Egypt: Every time Passover is celebrated, the Exodus events are made present to the memory of the believers so that they may conform their lives to them." —CCC 1363

Tuesday

In Sunday's Gospel reading from Luke 13:1-9, Jesus tells the parable of the barren fig tree. What do you think the meaning of this parable is? What are some things in your life that "choke" your spiritual life? What can you do to help bear more fruit in your faith life?

"You are my hope, Lord; my trust, God, from my youth."
—Psalm 71:5

Wednesday

In Sunday's video, the presenter mentions that many of the Jewish people were hiding behind the temple, saying that despite their sinful actions, they were "good enough" because of their adherence to temple rituals. What are some of the ways we merely go through the motions of our faith and settle for being "good enough"? How can you live your faith more fully and with conviction?

"The call for a sincere gift of self is the fullest way to realize our personal freedom."
—St. Teresa of Avila

Thursday

This Sunday's first and second readings both had to do with the Exodus story. Elsewhere in his letters, St. Paul compares sin to a "taskmaster" like the ones lording over the Israelite slaves in the Exodus story. In what ways does sin enslave us? How can you, especially during this season of Lent, turn away from sin and toward God?

"For freedom Christ has set us free; stand fast therefore, and do not submit again to a yoke of slavery....For you were called to freedom...only do not use your freedom as an opportunity for the flesh, but through love be servants of one another."
—Galatians 5:1, 13 (RSV)

Friday

In Sunday's second reading from the first letter of St. Paul to the Corinthians (10:1-6, 10-12), he reminds his listeners that "all" who came out of Egypt in the Old Testament experienced God's amazing graces, but that "most" of them still fell to great sin. In what ways have we failed to recognize the great gifts that God has given us?

> *"He is generous even to exhaustion; and what is most wonderful is, that he gives himself thus entirely, not once only, but every day, if we wish it. Every fresh Communion is a new gift which Jesus Christ makes of himself."*
>
> —St. Ignatius Loyola

Saturday

In Sunday's first reading from the Book of Exodus (3:1-8, 13-15), God says that "I have witnessed the affliction of my people in Egypt and have heard their cry of complaint against their slave drivers, so I know well what they are suffering." How can God understand our personal sufferings today? How can we entrust them to him?

> *"Or are you unaware that we who were baptized into Christ Jesus were baptized into his death? We were indeed buried with him through baptism into death, so that, just as Christ was raised from the dead by the glory of the Father, we too might live in newness of life."*
>
> —Romans 6:3-4

181

4TH SUNDAY OF LENT
⸱ YEAR C ⸱

A TALE OF TWO SONS

READINGS FOR THE FOURTH SUNDAY OF LENT

FIRST READING
- Joshua 5:9a, 10-12 -

The Lord said to Joshua, "Today I have removed the reproach of Egypt from you."

While the Israelites were encamped at Gilgal on the plains of Jericho, they celebrated the Passover on the evening of the fourteenth of the month. On the day after the Passover, they ate of the produce of the land in the form of unleavened cakes and parched grain. On that same day after the Passover, on which they ate of the produce of the land, the manna ceased. No longer was there manna for the Israelites, who that year ate of the yield of the land of Canaan.

RESPONSORIAL PSALM
- Psalm 34:2-3, 4-5, 6-7 -

R: **Taste and see the goodness of the Lord.**

I will bless the Lord at all times;
his praise shall be ever in my mouth.
Let my soul glory in the Lord;
the lowly will hear me and be glad.
R:

Glorify the Lord with me,
let us together extol his name.
I sought the Lord, and he answered me,
and delivered me from all my fears.
R:

Look to him that you may be radiant with joy,
and your faces may not blush with shame.
When the poor one called out, the Lord heard,
and from all his distress he saved him.
R:

SECOND READING

- 2 Corinthians 5:17-21-

Brothers and sisters: Whoever is in Christ is a new creation: the old things have passed away; behold new things have come. And all this is from God, who has reconciled us to himself through Christ and given us the ministry of reconciliation, namely, God was reconciling the world to himself in Christ, not counting their trespasses against them and entrusting to us the message of reconciliation. So we are ambassadors for Christ, as if God were appealing through us. We implore you on behalf of Christ, be reconciled to God. For our sake he made him to be sin who did not know sin, so that we might become the righteousness of God in him.

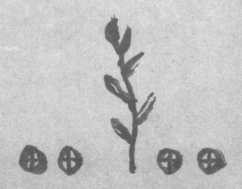

GOSPEL
- Luke 15:1-3, 11-32 -

Tax collectors and sinners were all drawing near to listen to Jesus, but the Pharisees and scribes began to complain, saying, "This man welcomes sinners and eats with them." So to them Jesus addressed this parable: "A man had two sons, and the younger son said to his father, 'Father give me the share of your estate that should come to me.' So the father divided the property between them. After a few days, the younger son collected all his belongings and set off to a distant country where he squandered his inheritance on a life of dissipation. When he had freely spent everything, a severe famine struck that country, and he found himself in dire need. So he hired himself out to one of the local citizens who sent him to his farm to tend the swine. And he longed to eat his fill of the pods on which the swine fed, but nobody gave him any. Coming to his senses he thought, 'How many of my father's hired workers have more than enough food to eat, but here am I, dying from hunger. I shall get up and go to my father and I shall say to him, "Father, I have sinned against heaven and against you. I no longer deserve to be called your son; treat me as you would treat one of your hired workers."' So he got up and went back to his father. While he was still a long way off, his father caught sight of him, and was filled with compassion. He ran to his son, embraced him and kissed him. His son said to him, 'Father, I have sinned against heaven and against you; I no longer deserve to be called your son.' But his father ordered his servants, 'Quickly bring the finest robe and put it on him; put a ring on his finger and sandals on his feet. Take the fattened calf and slaughter it. Then let us celebrate with a feast, because this son of mine was dead, and has come to life again; he was lost, and has been found.' Then the celebration began. Now the older son had been out in the field and, on his way back, as he neared the house, he heard the sound of music and dancing. He called one of the servants and asked what this might mean. The servant said to him, 'Your brother has returned and your father slaughtered the fattened calf because he has him back safe and sound.' He became angry, and when he refused to enter the house, his father came out and pleaded with him. He said to his father in reply, 'Look, all these years I served you and not once did I disobey your orders; yet you never gave me even a young goat to feast on with my friends. But when your son returns who swallowed up your property with prostitutes, for him you slaughter the fattened calf.' He said to him, 'My son, you are here with me always; everything I have is yours. But now we must celebrate and rejoice, because your brother was dead and has come to life again; he was lost and has been found.'"

Sunday

OPENING PRAYER

Out of the depths I call to you, Lord;
Lord, hear my cry!
May your ears be attentive to my cry for mercy.
If you, Lord, mark our sins,
Lord, who can stand?
But with you is found forgiveness
and so you are revered.

I wait with longing for the Lord,
my soul waits for his word.
My soul looks for the Lord
more than sentinels for daybreak.
More than sentinels for daybreak,
let Israel look for the Lord,
For with the Lord is kindness,
with him is full redemption,
And God will redeem Israel from all their sins.
Amen.

—Psalm 130

LECTIO DIVINA ✷ SACRED READING OF SCRIPTURE

Feel free to take notes on the video reflection in the space below.

LECTIO DIVINA ✷ MEDITATION

The presenter shared some of the historical background for this familiar story. What are some things about the story of the prodigal son that would have been shocking to Jesus' audience in the first century?

In this story the younger son looked for happiness by squandering his money in a "distant country" (Luke 15:13). What are some ways we look for happiness in things that don't really satisfy?

In the story we see that the older son served his father obediently, but without joy. In what ways have you ever viewed God as a master rather than a loving father?

How can we guard against this?

LECTIO DIVINA ✶ PRAYER & RESOLUTION

PRAYER: Take time now to consider your relationship with your heavenly Father. Prayerfully place yourself in the Gospel story. First imagine that you are the younger son leaving home, squandering your inheritance in a distant land, and ending up destitute, starving, and alone. How do you feel? What do you say to yourself? What do you do? Next imagine you are the older son dutifully working at home but not recognizing the love and generosity of your father. Now decide with which son you identify more at this point in your life. Put yourself in the position of that particular son and imagine the father coming out to meet you and inviting you into the feast. What would you say in response? How do you feel when your brother appears on the scene?

RESOLUTION: Just like the father in the parable, our heavenly Father comes out to us and invites us into his love. In prayer, talk to God about what he is inviting you to do to go deeper into your relationship with him this week.

> "When God runs toward us, we cannot keep silent, but with St. Paul we exclaim: Abba Pater, Father, my Father! For, though he is the creator of the universe, he doesn't mind our not using high-sounding titles, nor worry about our not acknowledging his greatness. He wants us to call him Father, he wants us to savor that word, our souls filling with joy." —St. Josemaria Escriva

189

Monday

In Sunday's first reading from the book of Joshua, the Lord tells Joshua and the Israelites that he has "removed the reproach of Egypt" from them (Joshua 5:9). In your prayer time, consider the reproach of sin that God has removed from you. Take time to thank him for his forgiveness.

"Come now, let us set things right, says the Lord: *Though your sins be like scarlet, they may become white as snow; though they be crimson red, they may become white as wool."* —Isaiah 1:18

Tuesday

Reread last Sunday's responsorial psalm from Psalm 34:2-7. As you meditate on these verses, ask God how he wants you to taste and see his goodness in a particular way this week.

"Which one of you would hand his son a stone when he asks for a loaf of bread, or a snake when he asks for a fish? If you then, who are wicked, know how to give good gifts to your children, how much more will your heavenly Father give good things to those who ask him." —Matthew 7:9-11

Wednesday

In Sunday's second reading from 2 Corinthians, St. Paul implores us to "be reconciled to God" (2 Corinthians 5:20). Ask God to show you if there is any unresolved sin in your life concerning which you need to be reconciled to him.

"'God created us without us: but he did not will to save us without us.' To receive his mercy, we must admit our faults....'If we confess our sins, he is faithful and just, and will forgive our sins.'"—CCC 1847

Thursday

Consider the father in last Sunday's Gospel reading of the prodigal son (Luke 15:1-3, 11-32). He ran to meet his younger son and welcome him home; he was quick to forgive, despite having been insulted and abandoned by his son. Prayerfully consider whether there is anyone who has offended you, either recently or in the past, whom you still need to forgive. Pray for the grace to forgive and let go of the hurt.

"If you forgive others their transgressions, your heavenly Father will forgive you. But if you do not forgive others, neither will your Father forgive your transgressions."—Matthew 6:14-15

Friday

Reread last Sunday's second reading from 2 Corinthians 5:17-21. St. Paul speaks of a "ministry of reconciliation"—ask God how he is calling you to participate in this ministry as an ambassador of Christ this week.

"Christ has no body now on earth but yours, no hands but yours, no feet but yours. Yours are the eyes through which to look out Christ's compassion to the world. Yours are the feet with which he is to go about doing good; yours are the hands with which he is to bless men now."

—St Teresa of Avila

Saturday

Consider the theme of repentance throughout last Sunday's readings, especially the second reading (2 Corinthians 5:17-21) and the Gospel reading (Luke 15:1-3, 11-32). Take some time in your prayer to make an examination of conscience based on the two sons in the Gospel reading: How have I squandered the gifts God has given me? How have I dishonored or insulted God? How have I removed myself from God's presence? How have I gone through the motions without being aware of God's love for me?

"Confession heals, confession justifies, confession grants pardon of sin; all hope consists in confession; in confession there is a chance for mercy."

—Romans 6:3-4

5TH SUNDAY OF LENT
ᘐ YEAR C ᘐ

MERCY AND CONVERSION

READINGS for the FIFTH SUNDAY of LENT

FIRST READING
- Isaiah 43:16-21 -

Thus says the Lord,/ who opens a way in the sea/ and a path in the mighty waters,/ who leads out chariots and horsemen,/ a powerful army,/ till they lie prostrate together, never to rise,/ snuffed out and quenched like a wick./ Remember not the events of the past,/ the things of long ago consider not;/ see, I am doing something new!/ Now it springs forth, do you not perceive it?/ In the desert I make a way,/ in the wasteland, rivers./ Will beasts honor me,/ jackals and ostriches,/ for I put water in the desert/ and rivers in the wasteland/ for my chosen people to drink,/ the people whom I formed for myself,/ that they might announce my praise.

RESPONSORIAL PSALM
- Psalm 126:1-2, 2-3, 4-5, 6 -

R: **The Lord has done great things for us; we are filled with joy.**

When the Lord brought back the captives of Zion,
we were like men dreaming.
Then our mouth was filled with laughter;
and our tongue with rejoicing.
R:

Then they said among the nations,
"The Lord has done great things for them."
The Lord has done great things for us;
we are glad indeed.
R:

Restore our fortunes, O Lord,
like the torrents in the southern desert.
Those that sow in tears
shall reap rejoicing.
R:

Although they go forth weeping,
carrying the seed to be sown,
they shall come back rejoicing,
carrying their sheaves.
R:

SECOND READING
- Philippians 3:8-14 -

Brothers and sisters: I consider everything as a loss because of the supreme good of knowing Christ Jesus my Lord. For his sake I have accepted the loss of all things and I consider them so much rubbish, that I may gain Christ and be found in him, not having any righteousness of my own based on the law but that which comes through faith in Christ, the righteousness from God, depending on faith to know him and the power of his resurrection and the sharing of his sufferings by being conformed to his death, if somehow I may attain the resurrection from the dead.

It is not that I have already taken hold of it or have already attained perfect maturity, but I continue my pursuit in hope that I may possess it, since I have indeed been taken possession of by Christ Jesus. Brothers and sisters, I for my part do not consider myself to have taken possession. Just one thing: forgetting what lies behind but straining forward to what lies ahead, I continue my pursuit toward the goal, the prize of God's upward calling, in Christ Jesus.

GOSPEL
- John 8:1-11 -

Jesus went to the Mount of Olives. But early in the morning he arrived again in the temple area, and all the people started coming to him, and he sat down and taught them. Then the scribes and the Pharisees brought a woman who had been caught in adultery and made her stand in the middle. They said to him, "Teacher, this woman was caught in the very act of committing adultery. Now in the law, Moses commanded us to stone such women. So what do you say?" They said this to test him, so that they could have some charge to bring against him. Jesus bent down and began to write on the ground with his finger. But when they continued asking him, he straightened up and said to them, "Let the one among you who is without sin be the first to throw a stone at her." Again he bent down and wrote on the ground. And in response, they went away one by one, beginning with the elders. So he was left alone with the woman before him. Then Jesus straightened up and said to her, "Woman, where are they? Has no one condemned you?" She replied, "No one, sir." Then Jesus said, "Neither do I condemn you. Go, and from now on do not sin anymore."

Sunday

OPENING PRAYER

Soul of Christ, sanctify me
Body of Christ, save me.
Blood of Christ, inebriate me.
Water from the side of Christ, wash me.
Passion of Christ, strengthen me.
O Good Jesus, hear me.
Within your wounds conceal me.
Do not permit me to be parted from you.
From the evil foe protect me.
At the hour of my death call me.
And bid me come to you,
to praise you with all your saints,
Forever and ever. Amen.

—Anima Christi

LECTIO DIVINA 🜂 SACRED READING OF SCRIPTURE

Feel free to take notes on the video reflection in the space below.

LECTIO DIVINA 🜂 MEDITATION

In this Gospel reading, Jesus' responses to the Pharisees and the woman caught in adultery reveal how he wants to respond to us and help us live our lives as his disciples.

How are the Pharisees trying to trap Jesus? How does Jesus' response to the Pharisees show his great wisdom?

Think of a time that you experienced sinfulness in your own life. How does Jesus' response to the woman reflect his mercy and the way Jesus desires to deal with your sinfulness?

LECTIO DIVINA PRAYER & RESOLUTION

PRAYER: Think of a sin that you have committed or an embarrassing weakness that you would not want others to know about. Now imagine yourself in the position of the woman in today's Gospel reading. Imagine that it is your sin that the Pharisees are revealing to the crowds and condemning. How would you feel in that situation? Then imagine Jesus approaching you with compassion and saying "Neither do I condemn you. Go and sin no more." How would you respond to Jesus' mercy? What would you say to him? How would you act differently?

RESOLUTION: Jesus offers the woman in today's Gospel reading—and all of us—both mercy and the challenge to "go and sin no more." Talk to God about one practical thing you could do this week to avoid a sin that troubles you and turn more readily to his mercy and grace.

"If self-knowledge and the thought of sin are not seasoned with the remembrance of the blood and hope for mercy, the result is bound to be confusion." —St. Catherine of Sienna

Monday

Sunday's Gospel reading about the woman caught in adultery focused our attention on God's mercy. Place yourself before a crucifix and spend a few minutes meditating upon Jesus' sacrifice to free us from our sins. What does the crucifix reveal about your sin? about the mercy of God? Spend some time entrusting yourself to Christ and his great mercy, and hand over to him anything in your life that needs healing and forgiveness.

"The human heart is converted by looking upon him whom our sins have pierced." —CCC 1432

Tuesday

Reread the second reading from the letter of St. Paul to the Philippians (3:8-14). How can you keep Jesus always in front of you as you live your life this week? How can you continue to pursue the goal St. Paul speaks about?

"I have competed well; I have finished the race; I have kept the faith. From now on the crown of righteousness awaits me, which the Lord, the just judge, will award to me on that day, and not only to me, but to all who have longed for his appearance." —2 Timothy 4:7-8

Wednesday

In the Sunday Gospel reading, we saw the Pharisees' willingness to judge and condemn the woman for her sin. Do you judge others and rush to judgment? If you do, ask God to help you change your behavior this week.

"Fear brings us only to justice as it is shown to sinners, but that is not the justice Jesus will have for those who love him." —St. Theresa of Lisieux

Thursday

Read the responsorial psalm from Sunday's reading, Psalm 126. As we saw in the Gospel reading, one of the most wonderful deeds that God can do in our lives is forgive our sins. What are some marvelous things God has done in your life? Spend some time in praise and thanksgiving to God for these gifts.

"Give thanks in all circumstances; for this is the will of God in Christ Jesus for you." —1 Thessalonians 5:18 (RSV)

Friday

Reread Sunday's first reading from the book of Isaiah (43:16-21). In what ways do you perceive God doing something new in your life? Give thanks for any signs of new life and growth you see.

> *"I came that they might have life and have it abundantly."*
>
> —John 10:10 (RSV)

Saturday

Once again place yourself before a crucifix and after thanking Jesus for the gift of his mercy, recall one specific passage from this week's readings that most touched you. Spend some time writing and in prayer around this passage.

"Most high, glorious God, enlighten the darkness of my heart and give me true faith, certain hope, and perfect charity, sense and knowledge, so that I may carry out your holy and true command. Amen."

—St. Francis of Assisi, Prayer Before the Crucifix

PALM SUNDAY
The passion of the lord
❧ YEAR C ❧

FAITHFULNESS UNDER PRESSURE

READINGS FOR PALM SUNDAY

FIRST READING
- Isaiah 50:4-7 -

The Lord GOD has given me/ a well-trained tongue,/ that I might know how to speak to the weary/ a word that will rouse them./ Morning after morning/ he opens my ear that I may hear;/ and I have not rebelled,/ have not turned back./ I gave my back to those who beat me,/ my cheek to those who plucked my beard;/ my face I did not shield/ from buffets and spitting./ The Lord God is my help,/ therefore I am not disgraced;/ I have set my face like flint,/ knowing that I shall not be put to shame.

RESPONSORIAL PSALM
- Psalm 22:8-9, 17-18, 19-20, 23-24 -

R: **My God, my God, why have you abandoned me?**

All who see me scoff at me;
they mock me with parted lips, they wag their heads:
"He relied on the LORD; let him deliver him,
let him rescue him, if he loves him."
R:

Indeed, many dogs surround me,
a pack of evildoers closes in upon me;
they have pierced my hands and my feet;
I can count all my bones.
R:

They divide my garments among them,
and for my vestures they cast lots.
But you, O LORD, be not far from me;
O my help, hasten to aid me.
R:

I will proclaim your name to my brethren;
in the midst of the assembly I will praise you:
"You who fear the LORD, praise him;
all you descendents of Jacob, give glory to him;
revere him, all you descendents of Israel!"
R:

SECOND READING
- Philippians 2:6-11 -

Christ Jesus, though he was in the form of God,/ did not regard equality with God/ something to be grasped./ Rather, he emptied himself,/ taking the form of a slave,/ coming in human likeness;/ and found human in appearance,/ he humbled himself,/ becoming obedient to the point of death,/ even death on a cross./ Because of this, God greatly exalted him/ and bestowed on him the name/ which is above every name,/ that at the name of Jesus/ every knee should bend,/ of those in heaven and on earth and under the earth,/ and every tongue confess that/ Jesus Christ is Lord,/ to the glory of God the Father.

GOSPEL
- Luke 22:14–23:56 -

[Shorter Form is indented in brackets]
(Narrator is in bold text)

**When the hour came, Jesus took his place at table
with the apostles. He said to them.**

"I have eagerly desired to eat this Passover with you before I suffer, for I tell you, I shall not eat it again until there is fulfillment in the kingdom of God."

Then he took a cup, gave thanks, and said,

"Take this and share it among yourselves; for I tell you that from this time on I shall not drink of the fruit of the vine until the kingdom of God comes."

**Then he took the bread, said a blessing, broke it,
and gave it to them, saying,**

"This is my body, which will be given for you; do this in memory of me."

And likewise the cup after they had eaten, saying,

*"This is the new covenant in my blood, which will be shed for you.
"And yet behold, the hand of the one who is to betray me is with me on the table; for the Son of Man indeed goes as it has been determined; but woe to that man by whom he is betrayed."*

**And they began to debate among themselves
who among them would do such a deed.**

Then an argument broke out among them about which of them should be regarded as the greatest. He said to them,

"The kings of the Gentiles lord it over them and those in authority over them are addressed as 'Benefactors'; but among you it shall not be so. Rather, let the greatest among you be as the youngest, and the leader as the servant. For who is greater: the one seated at table or the one who serves? Is it not the one seated at table? I am among you as the one who serves. It is you who have stood by me in my trials; and I confer a kingdom on you, just as my Father had conferred one on me, that you may eat and drink at my table in my kingdom; and you will sit on thrones judging the twelve tribes of Israel.

"Simon, Simon, behold Satan had demanded to sift all of you like wheat, but I have prayed that your own faith may not fail; and once you have turned back, you must strengthen your brothers."

He said to him,

"Lord, I am prepared to go to prison and to die with you."

But he replied,

"I tell you, Peter, before the cock crows this day, you will deny three times that you know me."

He said to them,

"When I sent you forth without a money bag or a sack or sandals, were you in need of anything?"

"No, nothing," they replied.
He said to them,

"But now one who has a money bag should take it, and likewise a sack, and one who does not have a sword should sell his cloak and buy one. For I tell you that this Scripture must be fulfilled in me, namely, He was counted among the wicked; and indeed what is written about me is coming to fulfillment."

Then they said,

"Lord, look, there are two swords here."

But he replied,

"It is enough!"

Then going out, he went, as was his custom, to the Mount of Olives, and the disciples followed him. When he arrived at the place he said to them,

"Pray that you may not undergo the test."

After withdrawing about a stone's throw from them
and kneeling, he prayed, saying,

*"Father, if you are willing, take this cup away from me; still,
not my will but yours be done."*

And to strengthen him an angel from heaven appeared to him. He was in
such agony and he prayed so fervently that his sweat became like drops of
blood falling on the ground. When he rose from prayer and returned to his
disciples, he found them sleeping from grief. He said to them,

"Why are you sleeping? Get up and pray that you may not undergo the test."

While he was still speaking, a crowd approached and in front was one of
the Twelve, a man named Judas.

He went up to Jesus to kiss him. Jesus said to him,

"Judas, are you betraying the Son of Man with a kiss?"

His disciples realized what was about to happen,
and they asked,

"Lord, shall we strike with a sword?"

And one of them struck the high priest's servant
and cut off his right ear.

But Jesus said in reply,

"Stop, no more of this!"

Then he touched the servant's ear and healed him.
And Jesus said to the chief priests and temple guards
and elders who had come for him,

*"Have you come out as against a robber, with swords and clubs? Day after day
I was with you in the temple area, and you did not seize me; but this is your
hour, the time for the power of darkness."*

After arresting him they led him away and took him into the house of the
high priest; Peter was following at a distance. They lit a fire in the middle
of the courtyard and sat around it, and Peter sat down with them. When a
maid saw him seated in the light, she looked intently at him and said,

"This man too was with him."

But he denied it saying,

"Woman, I do not know him."

A short while later someone else saw him and said,

"You too are one of them,"

but Peter answered,

"My friend, I am not."

About an hour later, still another insisted,

"Assuredly, this man too was with him, for he also is a Galilean."

But Peter said,

"My friend, I do not know what you are talking about."

Just as he was saying this, the cock crowed, and the Lord turned and looked at Peter; and Peter remembered the word of the Lord, how he had said to him,

**"Before the cock crows today,
you will deny me three times."
He went out and began to weep bitterly.
The men who held Jesus in custody were ridiculing and beating him. They blindfolded him and questioned him, saying,**

"Prophesy! Who is it that struck you?"

And they reviled him in saying many other things against him.

When day came the council of elders of the people met, both chief priests and scribes, and they brought him before their Sanhedrin. They said,

"If you are the Christ, tell us,"

but he replied to them,

"If I tell you, you will not believe, and if I question, you will not respond. But from this time on the Son of Man will be seated at the right hand of the power of God."

They all asked,

"Are you then the Son of God?"

He replied to them,

"You say that I am."

Then they said,

"What further need have we for testimony? We have heard it from his own mouth."

Then the whole assembly of them [The elders of the people, chief priests and scribes, arose and brought him [Jesus] before Pilate.

They brought charges against him, saying,

"We found this man misleading our people; he opposes the payment of taxes to Caesar and maintains that he is the Christ, a king."

Pilate asked him,

"Are you the king of the Jews?"

He said to him in reply,

"You say so."

Pilate then addressed the chief priests and the crowds,

"I find this man not guilty."

But they were adamant and said,

"He is inciting the people with his teaching throughout all Judea, from Galilee were he began even to here."

On hearing this Pilate asked if the man was a Galilean; and upon learning that he was under Herod's jurisdiction, he sent him to Herod who was in Jerusalem at that time. Herod was very glad to see Jesus; he had been wanting to see him for a long time, for he had heard about him and had been hoping to see him perform some sign. He questioned him at length, but he gave him no answer. The chief priests and scribes, meanwhile, stood by accusing him harshly. Herod and his soldiers treated him contemptuously and mocked him, and after clothing him in resplendent garb, he sent him back to Pilate. Herod and Pilate became friends that very day, even though they had been enemies formerly. Pilate then summoned the chief priests, the rulers, and the people and said to them,

"You brought this man to me and accused him of inciting the people to revolt. I have conducted my investigation in your presence and have not found this man guilty of the charges you have brought against him, nor did Herod, for he sent him back to us. So no capital crime has been committed by him. Therefore I shall have him flogged and then release him."

But all together they shouted out,

"Away with this man! Release Barabbas to us."

—Now Barabbas had been imprisoned for a rebellion that had taken place in the city and for murder.—
Again Pilate addressed them, still wishing to release Jesus, but they continued their shouting,

"Crucify him, Crucify him!"

Pilate addressed them a third time,

"What evil has this man done? I found him guilty of no capital crime. Therefore I shall have him flogged and then release him."

With loud shouts, however, they persisted in calling for his crucifixion, and their voices prevailed. The verdict of Pilate was that their demand should be granted.

So he released the man who had been imprisoned for rebellion and murder, for whom they asked, and he handed Jesus over to them to deal with as they wished.

As they led him they took hold of a certain Simon, a Cyrenian, who was coming in from the country; and after laying the cross on him, they made him carry it behind Jesus. A large crowd of people followed Jesus, including many women who mourned and lamented him.

Jesus turned to them and said,

"Daughters of Jerusalem, do not weep for me; weep instead for yourselves and for your children for indeed, the days are coming when people will say, 'Blessed are the barren, the wombs that never bore, and the breasts that never nursed.' At that time people will say to the mountains, 'Fall upon us!' and to the hills, 'Cover us!' For if these things are done when the wood is green what will happen when it is dry?"

Now two others, both criminals, were led away with him to be executed.

When they came to the place called the Skull, they crucified him and the criminals there, one on his right, the other on his left. Then Jesus said,

"Father, forgive them, they know not what they do."

They divided his garments by casting lots. The people stood by and watched; the rulers, meanwhile, sneered at him and said,

"He saved others, let him save himself if he is the chosen one, the Christ of God."

Even the soldiers jeered at him. As they approached to offer him wine they called out,

"If you are the King of the Jews, save yourself."

Above him there was an inscription that read, "This is the King of the Jews."

Now one of the criminals hanging there reviled Jesus, saying,

"Are you not the Christ? Save yourself and us."

The other, however, rebuking him, said in reply,

"Have you no fear of God, for you are subject to the same condemnation? And indeed, we have been condemned justly, for the sentence we received corresponds to our crimes, but this man has done nothing criminal."

Then he said,

"Jesus, remember me when you come into your kingdom."

He replied to him,

"Amen I say to you, today you will be with me in Paradise."

It was now about noon and darkness came over the whole land until three in the afternoon because of an eclipse of the sun. Then the veil of the temple was torn down the middle. Jesus cried out in a loud voice,

"Father, into your hands I commend my spirit;"

and when he had said this he breathed his last.

(Here all kneel and pause for short time.)

The centurion who witnessed what had happened glorified God and said,

"This man was innocent beyond doubt."

When all the people who had gathered for this spectacle saw what had happened, they returned home beating their breasts; but all his acquaintances stood at a distance, including the women who had followed him from Galilee and saw these events.]

Now there was a virtuous and righteous man named Joseph who, though he was a member of the council, had not consented to their plan of action. He came from the Jewish town of Arimethea and was awaiting the kingdom of God.

He went to Pilate and asked for the body of Jesus. After he had taken the body down, he wrapped it in a linen cloth and laid him in a rock-hewn tomb in which no one had yet been buried. It was the day of preparation, and the Sabbath was about to begin.

The women who had come from Galilee with him followed behind, and when they had seen the tomb and the way in which his body was laid in it, they returned and prepared spices and perfumed oils.

Then they rested on the Sabbath according to the commandment.

Sunday

OPENING PRAYER

Look down upon me good and gentle Jesus,
while before thy face I humbly kneel
and with burning soul pray and beseech thee
to fix deep in my heart lively sentiments of faith,
hope, and charity, true contrition for my sins
and a firm purpose of amendment,
while I contemplate with great love and tender pity
thy five wounds, pondering over them within me
and calling to mind the words which David,
Thy prophet said of thee, my Jesus,
"They have pierced my hands and my feet,
they have numbered all my bones." Amen.

—Prayer Before a Crucifix

LECTIO DIVINA ⚘ SACRED READING OF SCRIPTURE

Feel free to take notes on the video reflection in the space below.

LECTIO DIVINA ⚘ MEDITATION

The presenter, Father John Riley, discussed how we find different roles in today's Gospel reading of the Passion story, some good and some bad. He mentioned characters who proved to be unfaithful during Christ's passion and others who serve as models we are called to emulate.

In the video, what characters and roles were described as part of the Passion story?

What additional roles did other characters play in the Passion narrative?

The Mass makes the events of Passion Week spiritually present to us—as the *Catechism of the Catholic Church* teaches, the Mass is the "making present and the sacramental offering of [Christ's] unique sacrifice" (CCC 1362). We are called to play an active role in this memorial of the Passion.

Consider again the various roles we've discussed and the characters we listed at the beginning.

What role(s) do you think you have played in the past?

What character do you identify with the most at this point in your life? Why?

LECTIO DIVINA 🌿 PRAYER & RESOLUTION

PRAYER: In this study you have discussed the various roles in the Passion narrative, and you have considered with which character you can relate the most. Now in prayer, enter into the Passion narrative in your chosen role—the character from the Passion with whom you identify the most. Reread the parts of the Passion narrative in which your character appears and imagine being that person. How do you feel playing this part? How do you react to the events taking place? What do you say as the events unfold? Now imagine that Jesus sees you. What do you think he would say to you? What would you say to him?

RESOLUTION: Imagine that you are at the foot of the cross, gazing up at our crucified Lord. What are one or two practical things you can do this week to keep in mind the Passion events and remain a faithful follower of our Lord in the face of your daily challenges?

"Yet it was our infirmities that he bore, our sufferings that he endured, while we thought of him as stricken, as one smitten by God and afflicted. But he was pierced for our offenses, crushed for our sins, upon him was the chastisement that makes us whole, by his stripes we were healed." —Isaiah 53:4-5

Monday

Last Sunday's first reading from the prophet Isaiah describes courage in the face of persecution and ends with the verse "The Lord God is my help, therefore I am not disgraced; I have set my face like flint, knowing that I shall not be put to shame" (Isaiah 50:7). For what current challenge in your life do you need to "set your face like flint"? Pray today for the grace to trust in God to provide the help you need.

"The Lord is my light and my salvation; whom do I fear? The Lord is my life's refuge; of whom am I afraid?" —Psalm 27:1

Tuesday

The response for last Sunday's responsorial psalm was, "My God, my God, why have you abandoned me?" (Psalm 22:2). Even though the psalmist trusts God and his mighty strength (Psalm 22:20, 23-24), he feels abandoned by God in times of trouble. When in your life have you felt abandoned by God? Looking back, how did God make his presence known even in that hard time?

"But I cry out to you, Lord; in the morning my prayer comes before you. Why do you reject me, Lord? Why hide your face from me?" —2 Timothy 4:7-8

Wednesday

Consider last Sunday's second reading from Philippians 2:6-11. St. Paul tells us that Jesus "did not regard equality with God something to be grasped. Rather…he humbled himself, becoming obedient to the point of death." If Jesus, who is God, did not exploit his divinity for gain but rather humbled himself for our sake, then in what way is God calling you to humble yourself for the sake of others this week?

"Humility does not disturb or disquiet or agitate, however great it may be; it comes with peace, delight, and calm….The pain of genuine humility doesn't agitate or afflict the soul; rather, this humility expands it and enables it to serve God more." ——St Teresa of Avila

Thursday

Reread last Sunday's first reading from Isaiah 50:4-7. Consider the people in your daily life; is there anyone who's weary and needs a word to rouse them, as the prophet says? How can you share the Word of God with that person this week with patience and charity?

"Encourage yourselves daily while it is still 'today,' so that none of you may grow hardened by the deceit of sin."
—Hebrews 3:13

Friday

Reread the portion of last Sunday's Gospel reading found in Luke 23:44-49. Take some time to meditate on this account of Christ's death. What does it mean that the Son of God died for you, specifically?

"God loves each of us as if there were only one of us."

—St. Augustine

Saturday

In last Sunday's Gospel reading, we hear Jesus praying, "Father, if you are willing, take this cup away from me; still, not my will but yours be done" (Luke 22:42). In what way might God be calling you to surrender your will more to his?

"Lord what wilt thou have me do? Behold the true sign of a totally perfect soul: when one has reached the point of giving up his will so completely that he no longer seeks, expects, or desires to do ought but that which God wills."

—St. Bernard

FROM SORROW TO JOY

READINGS FOR EASTER SUNDAY

FIRST READING
- Acts 10:34a, 37-43 -

Peter proceeded to speak and said: "You know what has happened all over Judea, beginning in Galilee after the baptism that John preached how God anointed Jesus of Nazareth with the Holy Spirit and power. He went about doing good and healing all those oppressed by the devil, for God was with him. We are witnesses of all that he did both in the country of the Jews and in Jerusalem. They put him to death by hanging him on a tree. This man God raised on the third day and granted that he be visible, not to all the people, but to us, the witnesses chosen by God in advance, who ate and drank with him after he rose from the dead. He commissioned us to preach to the people and testify that he is the one appointed by God as judge of the living and the dead. To him all the prophets bear witness, that everyone who believes in him will receive forgiveness of sins through his name."

RESPONSORIAL PSALM
- Psalm 118:1-2, 16-17, 22-23 -

R: **This is the day the Lord has made; let us rejoice and be glad.**
or R: **Alleluia**

Give thanks to the LORD, for he is good,
for his mercy endures forever.
Let the house of Israel say,
"His mercy endures forever."
R:

"The right hand of the LORD has struck with power;
the right hand of the LORD is exalted.
I shall not die, but live,
and declare the works of the LORD."
R:

The stone which the builders rejected
has become the cornerstone.
By the LORD has this been done;
it is wonderful in our eyes.
R:

SECOND READING
- Colossians 3:1-4 -

Brothers and sisters: If then you were raised with Christ, seek what is above, where Christ is seated at the right hand of God. Think of what is above, not of what is on earth. For you have died, and your life is hidden with Christ in God. When Christ your life appears, then you too will appear with him in glory.

OPTIONAL SECOND READING
- 1 Corinthians 5:6b-8 -

Brothers and sisters: Do you not know that a little yeast leavens all the dough? Clear out the old yeast, so that you may become a fresh batch of dough, inasmuch as you are unleavened. For our paschal lamb, Christ, has been sacrificed. Therefore, let us celebrate the feast, not with the old yeast, the yeast of malice and wickedness, but with the unleavened bread of sincerity and truth.

GOSPEL
- John 20:1-9 -

On the first day of the week, Mary of Magdala came to the tomb early in the morning, while it was still dark, and saw the stone removed from the tomb. So she ran and went to Simon Peter and to the other disciple whom Jesus loved, and told them, "They have taken the Lord from the tomb, and we don't know where they put him." So Peter and the other disciple went out and came to the tomb. They both ran, but the other disciple ran faster than Peter and arrived at the tomb first; he bent down and saw the burial cloths there, but did not go in. When Simon Peter arrived after him, he went into the tomb and saw the burial cloths there, and the cloth that had covered his head, not with the burial cloths but rolled up in a separate place. Then the other disciple also went in, the one who had arrived at the tomb first, and he saw and believed. For they did not yet understand the Scripture that he had to rise from the dead.

Sunday

OPENING PRAYER

Rejoice, heavenly powers! Sing, choirs of angels!
Exult, all creation around God's throne!
Jesus Christ, our King, is risen!
Sound the trumpet of salvation!

Rejoice, O earth, in shining splendor,
radiant in the brightness of your King!
Christ has conquered! Glory fills you!
Darkness vanishes forever!

Rejoice, O Mother Church! Exult in glory!
The risen Savior shines upon you!
Let this place resound with joy,
echoing the mighty song of all God's people!

—Exsultet

LECTIO DIVINA ❧ SACRED READING OF SCRIPTURE

Feel free to take notes on the video reflection in the space below.

LECTIO DIVINA ❧ MEDITATION

In his discussion of the Lord's Day, the presenter refers to the New Creation described at the beginning of the Gospel of John. How does this prologue of the Gospel of John connect to the story of creation from Genesis?

Why does John make this connection?

Christians gather on the Lord's Day to celebrate the greatest of God's saving works. Why do Christians gather on Sunday for worship when the Sabbath for the Jews was on Saturday?

How is this gathering meant to remind us of God's work in our own lives?

LECTIO DIVINA ⟡ PRAYER & RESOLUTION

PRAYER: Place yourself in the footsteps of St. Mary Magdalene on Easter morning. You go to the tomb to anoint the dead body of the Master you loved and followed for so long. You approach the tomb in darkness and in great sorrow, remembering the suffering you watched Jesus endure on Good Friday. Now, as you encounter the resurrected Lord, what do you feel as you become aware that Jesus is truly alive and risen?

RESOLUTION: As you imagine being present at the joy of the Resurrection, ask Jesus what he would have you do with your life from this point on. Think of one "dark" or difficult area of your life, and ask him how you can replace that area of darkness with the light of the Resurrection or transform an area of sorrow into joy.

"Now let the heavens be joyful, Let earth her song begin; Let the round world keep triumph, And all that is therein; Invisible and visible, Their notes let all things blend, For Christ the Lord is risen; Our joy that hath no end." —St. John of Damascus

Monday

This week the Catholic Church celebrates the Easter Octave, a weeklong celebration of the Feast of Easter. As you continue to celebrate your Easter feast, reflect on the immense gift of the Resurrection of the Lord and how we would not be Christians without it.

"And he departed from our sight that we might return to our heart, and there find him. For he departed, and behold, he is here."—St. Augustine

Tuesday

The Gospel passage states that the disciples "did not yet understand the Scripture that he had to rise from the dead" (John 20:9). Think of one aspect of the faith you have a difficult time understanding, and ask Jesus to illumine your mind and heart so that you can come to understand the fullness of the faith.

"Make no mistake: If he rose at all it was as his body; if the cells' dissolution did not reverse, the molecules reknit, the amino acids rekindle, the Church will fall." —John Updike

Wednesday

Reread the first reading from the Acts of the Apostles (Acts 10:34a, 37-43). In this reading, Peter states that Jesus chose to show himself to witnesses chosen by God, the apostles, so that they may preach the message of Jesus to all the ends of the earth. Take some time to thank God for the gift of the Church and the courage of the apostles in spreading the message of Christ in the midst of immense persecution.

"Do not abandon yourselves to despair. We are the Easter people and hallelujah is our song."—St Teresa of Avila

Thursday

In the second reading from St. Paul to the Colossians, Paul tells the faithful to "seek what is above" (Colossians 3:2). What does this mean for your life right now? How are you "seeking what is above" in your day-to-day activities?

"Faith in the resurrection of Jesus says that there is a future for every human being; the cry for unending life which is a part of the person is indeed answered... God exists: that is the real message of Easter. Anyone who even begins to grasp what this means also knows what it means to be redeemed."
—Pope Benedict XVI

Friday

In the Gospel reading from St. John, Peter arrives at the tomb second, yet is the first to enter. Peter's doubt and confusion holds him back initially, yet he is still the one chosen to lead the disciples into the tomb to encounter the crux of their faith: the Resurrection. In the same way, the Chair of Peter—the Pope—is called to lead all faithful today to an encounter with Jesus through the faith. Take some time reflecting on how you can better follow the wisdom and guidance of the Holy Father in your life.

> *"Sunday is the pre-eminent day for the liturgical assembly, when the faithful gather "to listen to the word of God and take part in the Eucharist, thus calling to mind the Passion, Resurrection, and glory of the Lord Jesus, and giving thanks to God who 'has begotten them again, by the resurrection of Jesus Christ from the dead' unto a living hope."*
>
> —St. Augustine

Saturday

As you look back at your week, reflect on the ways you celebrated and rejoiced in the Resurrection of our Lord. What more can you do this Easter season to continually reflect on the gift of the Resurrection in your life?

"'Why do you seek the living one among the dead? He is not here, but he has been raised."
—Luke 24:5-6

2ND SUNDAY OF EASTER
DIVINE MERCY SUNDAY
ᘒ YEAR C ᘒ

TWO SIDES OF CHRIST'S LOVE

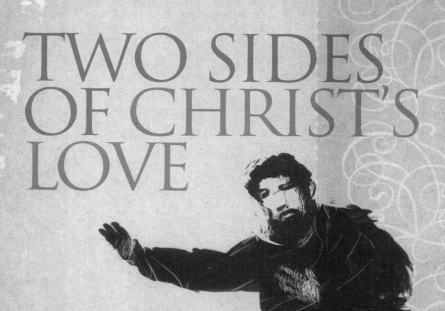

READINGS FOR THE SECOND SUNDAY OF EASTER

FIRST READING
- Acts 5:12-16 -

Many signs and wonders were done among the people at the hands of the apostles. They were all together in Solomon's portico. None of the others dared to join them, but the people esteemed them. Yet more than ever, believers in the Lord, great numbers of men and women, were added to them. Thus they even carried the sick out into the streets and laid them on cots and mats so that when Peter came by, at least his shadow might fall on one or another of them. A large number of people from the towns in the vicinity of Jerusalem also gathered, bringing the sick and those disturbed by unclean spirits, and they were all cured.

RESPONSORIAL PSALM
- Psalm 118:2-4, 13-15, 22-24 -

R: **Give thanks to the Lord, for he is good, his love is everlasting.**
or R: **Alleluia**

Let the house of Israel say,
"His mercy endures forever."
Let the house of Aaron say,
"His mercy endures forever."
Let those who fear the LORD say,
"His mercy endures forever."
R:

I was hard pressed and was falling,
but the LORD helped me.
My strength and my courage is the LORD,
and he has been my savior.
The joyful shout of victory
in the tents of the just:
R:

The stone which the builders rejected
has become the cornerstone.
By the LORD has this been done;
it is wonderful in our eyes.
This is the day the LORD has made;
let us be glad and rejoice in it.
R:

SECOND READING
- Revelation 1:9-11a, 12-13, 17-19 -

*I, John, your brother, who share with you the distress,
the kingdom, and the endurance we have in Jesus, found
myself on the island called Patmos because I proclaimed
God's word and gave testimony to Jesus. I was caught
up in spirit on the Lord's day and heard behind me a
voice as loud as a trumpet, which said, "Write on a scroll
what you see." Then I turned to see whose voice it was
that spoke to me, and when I turned, I saw seven gold
lampstands and in the midst of the lampstands one like
a son of man, wearing an ankle-length robe, with a gold
sash around his chest.*

*When I caught sight of him, I fell down at his feet as
though dead. He touched me with his right hand and
said, "Do not be afraid. I am the first and the last, the one
who lives. Once I was dead, but now I am alive forever
and ever. I hold the keys to death and the netherworld.
Write down, therefore, what you have seen, and what is
happening, and what will happen afterwards."*

GOSPEL
- John 20:19-31 -

On the evening of that first day of the week, when the doors were locked, where the disciples were, for fear of the Jews, Jesus came and stood in their midst and said to them, "Peace be with you." When he had said this, he showed them his hands and his side. The disciples rejoiced when they saw the Lord. Jesus said to them again, "Peace be with you. As the Father has sent me, so I send you." And when he had said this, he breathed on them and said to them, "Receive the Holy Spirit. Whose sins you forgive are forgiven them, and whose sins you retain are retained."

Thomas, called Didymus, one of the Twelve, was not with them when Jesus came. So the other disciples said to him, "We have seen the Lord." But he said to them, "Unless I see the mark of the nails in his hands and put my finger into the nailmarks and put my hand into his side, I will not believe."

Now a week later his disciples were again inside and Thomas was with them. Jesus came, although the doors were locked, and stood in their midst and said, "Peace be with you." Then he said to Thomas, "Put your finger here and see my hands, and bring your hand and put it into my side, and do not be unbelieving, but believe." Thomas answered and said to him, "My Lord and my God!" Jesus said to him, "Have you come to believe because you have seen me? Blessed are those who have not seen and have believed." Now Jesus did many other signs in the presence of his disciples that are not written in this book. But these are written that you may come to believe that Jesus is the Christ, the Son of God, and that through this belief you may have life in his name.

Sunday

OPENING PRAYER

O Lord,
show your mercy to me and gladden my heart.
I am like the man on the way to Jericho
who was overtaken by robbers,
wounded, and left for dead:
O good Samaritan, come to my aid.
I am like the sheep that went astray:
O good shepherd, seek me out and bring me home
in accord with your will.
Let me dwell in your house all the days of my life
and praise you forever and ever with those who are there.
Amen.

—Prayer for Mercy by St. Jerome

LECTIO DIVINA 🕭 SACRED READING OF SCRIPTURE

Feel free to take notes on the video reflection in the space below.

LECTIO DIVINA 🕭 MEDITATION

The presenter discusses the two sides of Christ's love. What are these two sides, and how do we see Jesus demonstrating both of them in today's Gospel reading?

In what ways do you see Jesus confronting you with both his truth and his mercy in your own life?

How do you commonly react to being confronted with the truth of sin?

How do you commonly react to being confronted with God's mercy?

LECTIO DIVINA 🔹 PRAYER & RESOLUTION

PRAYER: **Put yourself into today's Gospel reading. Imagine that you are in the upper room with the disciples. Jesus appears to you and shows you the wounds in his hands and in his side—these are the effects of your sins. How do you feel? What do you say to Jesus? Now imagine that Jesus extends his hands toward you and says, "Peace be with you." How do you feel? How would you respond? What do you do when you hear those words?**

RESOLUTION: **Through the Sacrament of Reconciliation we have direct access to the mission of forgiveness which the Father gave to Jesus, and which Jesus shared with the apostles. Make plans to go to Confession as soon as you can. In preparation, prayerfully ask God to reveal any hidden areas of sin in your life and help you to make a good confession.**

"How happy I am to see myself imperfect and be in need of God's mercy." —St. Theresa of Lisieux

Monday

In the second reading from last Sunday, St. John refers to his exile on Patmos. Are there any areas in your life where you risk a type of exile or ostracism for bearing witness to Jesus? Take time to pray for the wisdom and courage to handle these situations in the way God wants you to.

"After recalling the apostles, they had them flogged, ordered them to stop speaking in the name of Jesus, and dismissed them. So they left the presence of the Sanhedrin, rejoicing that they had been found worthy to suffer dishonor for the sake of the name. And all day long, both at the temple and in their homes, they did not stop teaching and proclaiming the Messiah, Jesus."
—Acts 5:40-42 (NABRE)

Tuesday

Consider the description of the signs and wonders worked by the apostles in last Sunday's first reading. Put yourself into this reading: What would it be like to witness those miracles in the early days of the Church in Jerusalem? Our bishops are the successors of the apostles—take some time during prayer today to pray for your bishop.

"Wherever the bishop shall appear, there let the multitude also be; even as, wherever Jesus Christ is, there is the Catholic Church."
—St. Ignatius of Antioch

Wednesday

In last Sunday's Gospel reading we hear about Thomas not believing that the rest of the disciples had seen the risen Lord until he sees Jesus with his own eyes. Jesus then tells the disciples, "Blessed are those who have not seen and have believed." Do you identify with Thomas' insistence on seeing before believing? Why or why not?

"Faith is the realization of what is hoped for and evidence of things not seen."—Hebrews 11:1

Thursday

Last Sunday's Gospel reading talks about peace, or shalom in Hebrew. In the video, the presenter discussed how this peace describes right relationship and covenant friendship. Is there anyone in your life with whom you are not at peace in this deeper sense? In your prayer time, bring this person to God and ask him for healing in this situation.

"Therefore, if you bring your gift to the altar, and there recall that your brother has anything against you, leave your gift there at the altar, go first and be reconciled with your brother, and then come and offer your gift."
—Matthew 5:23-24

Friday

In the second reading from last Sunday, St. John sees Jesus in all his glory. Put yourself into this story—imagine hearing the voice like trumpets and turning around to see the one like a son of man. How would you feel? What would you do or say?

> *"The glory of God is man fully alive, and the life of man is the vision of God."*
>
> —St. Irenaeus

Saturday

Last Sunday's responsorial psalm repeats the phrase "His mercy endures forever." In what ways have you experienced God's enduring mercy this week?

> *"Even if the sins of the soul are dark as night, when the sinner turns to my mercy he gives me the greatest praise and is the glory of my passion."*
>
> —St. Faustina Kowalska

3RD SUNDAY OF EASTER
~ YEAR C ~

DO YOU LOVE ME?

READINGS FOR THE THIRD SUNDAY OF EASTER

FIRST READING
- Acts 5:27-32, 40-41 -

When the captain and the court officers had brought the apostles in and made them stand before the Sanhedrin, the high priest questioned them, "We gave you strict orders, did we not, to stop teaching in that name? Yet you have filled Jerusalem with your teaching and want to bring this man's blood upon us." But Peter and the apostles said in reply, "We must obey God rather than men. The God of our ancestors raised Jesus, though you had him killed by hanging him on a tree. God exalted him at his right hand as leader and savior to grant Israel repentance and forgiveness of sins. We are witnesses of these things, as is the Holy Spirit whom God has given to those who obey him."

The Sanhedrin ordered the apostles to stop speaking in the name of Jesus, and dismissed them. So they left the presence of the Sanhedrin, rejoicing that they had been found worthy to suffer dishonor for the sake of the name.

RESPONSORIAL PSALM
- Psalm 30:2, 4, 5-6, 11-13 -

R: **I will praise you, Lord, for you have rescued me.** or R: **Alleluia**

I will extol you, O Lord, for you drew me clear
and did not let my enemies rejoice over me.
O Lord, you brought me up from the netherworld;
you preserved me from among those going down into the pit.
R:

Sing praise to the Lord, you his faithful ones,
and give thanks to his holy name.
For his anger lasts but a moment;
a lifetime, his good will.
At nightfall, weeping enters in,
but with the dawn, rejoicing.
R:

Hear, O Lord, and have pity on me;
O Lord, be my helper.
You changed my mourning into dancing;
O Lord, my God, forever will I give you thanks.
R:

SECOND READING
- Revelation 5:11-14 -

I, John, looked and heard the voices of many angels who surrounded the throne and the living creatures and the elders. They were countless in number, and they cried out in a loud voice: "Worthy is the Lamb that was slain/ to receive power and riches, wisdom and strength,/ honor and glory and blessing."/ Then I heard every creature in heaven and on earth and under the earth and in the sea, everything in the universe, cry out: "To the one who sits on the throne and to the Lamb/ be blessing and honor, glory and might,/ forever and ever."/ The four living creatures answered, "Amen," and the elders fell down and worshiped.

GOSPEL
- John 21:1-19 -

[When "Shorter Form" is used, the indented text in brackets is omitted]

At that time, Jesus revealed himself to his disciples at the Sea of Tiberias. He revealed himself in this way. Together were Simon Peter, Thomas called Didymus, Nathanael from Cana in Galilee, Zebedee's sons, and two others of his disciples. Simon Peter said to them, "I am going fishing." They said to him, "We also will come with you." So they went out and got into the boat, but that night they caught nothing. When it was already dawn, Jesus was standing on the shore; but the disciples did not realize that it was Jesus. Jesus said to them, "Children, have you caught anything to eat?" They answered him, "No." So he said to them, "Cast the net over the right side of the boat and you will find something." So they cast it, and were not able to pull it in because of the number of fish. So the disciple whom Jesus loved said to Peter, "It is the Lord." When Simon Peter heard that it was the Lord, he tucked in his garment, for he was lightly clad, and jumped into the sea. The other disciples came in the boat, for they were not far from the shore, only about a hundred yards, dragging the net with the fish. When they climbed out on shore, they saw a charcoal fire with fish on it and bread. Jesus said to them, "Bring some of the fish you just caught." So Simon Peter went over and dragged the net ashore full of one hundred fifty-three large fish. Even though there were so many, the net was not torn. Jesus said to them, "Come, have breakfast." And none of the disciples dared to ask him, "Who are you?" because they realized it was the Lord. Jesus came over and took the bread and gave it to them, and in like manner the fish. This was now the third time Jesus was revealed to his disciples after being raised from the dead.

[When they had finished the breakfast, Jesus said to Simon Peter, "Simon, son of John, do you love me more than these?" Simon Peter answered him, "Yes, Lord, you know that I love you." Jesus said to him, "Feed my lambs." He then said to Simon Peter a second time, "Simon, son of John, do you love me?" Simon Peter answered him, "Yes, Lord, you know that I love you." Jesus said to him, "Tend my sheep." Jesus said to him the third time, "Simon, son of John, do you love me?" Peter was distressed that Jesus had said to him a third time, "Do you love me?" and he said to him, "Lord, you know everything; you know that I love you." Jesus said to him, "Feed my sheep. Amen, amen, I say to you, when you were younger, you used to dress yourself and go where you wanted; but when you grow old, you will stretch out your hands, and someone else will dress you and lead you where you do not want to go." He said this signifying by what kind of death he would glorify God. And when he had said this, he said to him, "Follow me."]

Sunday

OPENING PRAYER

Dear Lord, you are always waiting with open arms to welcome us back when we fall away from you. Give us the grace to be like Peter, who ran to you to seek reconciliation. Help pick us up as often as we fall, and assist us in times of temptation and weakness. Be with us as you were with your disciples and make us ready to accept the overabundance of your gifts, like the overabundance of fish that you blessed the fishing apostles with. Help us to remain always near you. We ask this through Jesus Christ our Lord. Amen.

LECTIO DIVINA ✒ SACRED READING OF SCRIPTURE

Feel free to take notes on the video reflection in the space below.

LECTIO DIVINA ✒ MEDITATION

In the Gospel, according to the presenter, why does Peter use a different term for the word "love" than Jesus does?

Why does Jesus ask Peter three times if he loves him? What in the Gospel story might this be related to?

This week's first reading from the Acts of the Apostles shows us that Peter eventually gave Jesus "agape" love. How can Jesus transform the small things we are able to give him into great things?

LECTIO DIVINA ❧ PRAYER & RESOLUTION

PRAYER: Imagine that you were one of the disciples in today's Gospel scene. You have followed Jesus, learned from him, walked with him. But now imagine he pulls you aside and asks you the question that he asked Peter that day, "Do you love me?" What goes through your mind, knowing that Jesus will know your heart and the truthfulness of your answer? How would you respond? Are you willing to "agape" Jesus—to love Jesus with a total, unconditional, self-giving love? If, in truth, you would answer as Peter did with a "philia" love, what do you think Jesus would say to you in response?

RESOLUTION: Ask Jesus to show you one or two things in your life that might be holding you back from loving him with your whole heart, giving him that agape love. If you (like Peter) can't love God like this yet, ask him for the grace to be able to "agape" him, and trust in the meantime that he will accept your "philia" love as he did Peter's.

"If you are what you should be, you will set the whole world ablaze!"
—St. Catherine of Sienna

Monday

In Sunday's Gospel reading, Jesus asks Peter, "Do you love me with all that you are?" To which Peter answers, in essence, "You know I am your close friend." In some sense, Peter represents all of us. How would you answer Jesus' question?

> "We become what we love and who we love shapes what we become."
>
> —St. Clare of Assisi

Tuesday

St. Catherine Labouré lived in France in the 1800s. She saw a miraculous vision of the Blessed Mother, who was wearing different rings on her fingers, most of which were giving off beautiful rays of light over the world. These, she was told, represented God's graces. When the saint asked why not all of the rings were giving off light, Mary responded, "Those are the graces for which people forget to ask." Like the disciples with their surprising catch of fish, what do you need God's help with that you might never have asked him for?

> "You pay God a compliment by asking great things of him."
>
> —St. Teresa of Avila

Wednesday

What is one practical way that you can better love Jesus today?

_____

_____

_____

_____

_____

_____

"You can learn to speak by speaking, to study by studying, to run by running, to work by working, and just so, you learn to love by loving." —Hebrews 11:1

Thursday

On Holy Thursday, Peter denied Jesus three times. In Sunday's Gospel reading, he runs to Jesus for reconciliation. How do we respond when we've sinned against Jesus?

_____

_____

_____

_____

_____

_____

_____

_____

"Late have I loved you, O Beauty ever ancient, ever new, late have I loved you!"
—St. Augustine

Friday

In Sunday's first reading, taken from the Acts of the Apostles, Peter is finally willing to love Jesus in the way that Jesus desired. He is willing to suffer for Jesus and goes so far as to call it a privilege. Think of a time when you've had the privilege of suffering for Jesus.

> "The proof of love is in the works. Where love exists it works great things, but when it ceases to act, it ceases to exist."
> —Pope St. Gregory the Grea

Saturday

In Sunday's Gospel reading, Peter is not willing to give Jesus everything, but he does give him something—his philia love. Do you fail to give Jesus anything because you cannot give him everything? What is one small "yes" you can give to Jesus today?

> "Teach us to give and not count the cost."
> —St. Ignatius of Loyola

4TH SUNDAY OF EASTER
YEAR C

UNITED AS ONE FLOCK

READINGS FOR THE FOURTH SUNDAY OF EASTER

FIRST READING
- Acts 13:14, 43-52 -

Paul and Barnabas continued on from Perga and reached Antioch in Pisidia. On the Sabbath they entered the synagogue and took their seats. Many Jews and worshipers who were converts to Judaism followed Paul and Barnabas, who spoke to them and urged them to remain faithful to the grace of God.

On the following Sabbath almost the whole city gathered to hear the word of the Lord. When the Jews saw the crowds, they were filled with jealousy and with violent abuse contradicted what Paul said. Both Paul and Barnabas spoke out boldly and said, "It was necessary that the word of God be spoken to you first, but since you reject it and condemn yourselves as unworthy of eternal life, we now turn to the Gentiles. For so the Lord has commanded us, I have made you a light to the Gentiles, that you may be an instrument of salvation to the ends of the earth."

The Gentiles were delighted when they heard this and glorified the word of the Lord. All who were destined for eternal life came to believe, and the word of the Lord continued to spread through the whole region. The Jews, however, incited the women of prominence who were worshipers and the leading men of the city, stirred up a persecution against Paul and Barnabas, and expelled them from their territory. So they shook the dust from their feet in protest against them, and went to Iconium. The disciples were filled with joy and the Holy Spirit.

RESPONSORIAL PSALM
- Psalm 100:1-2, 3, 5 -

R: **We are his people, the sheep of his flock.**
or R: **Alleluia**

Sing joyfully to the LORD, all you lands;
serve the LORD with gladness;
come before him with joyful song.
R:

Know that the LORD is God;
he made us, his we are;
his people, the flock he tends.
R:

The LORD is good:
his kindness endures forever,
and his faithfulness, to all generations.
R:

SECOND READING
- Revelation 7:9, 14b-17 -

I, John, had a vision of a great multitude, which no one could count, from every nation, race, people, and tongue. They stood before the throne and before the Lamb, wearing white robes and holding palm branches in their hands.

Then one of the elders said to me, "These are the ones who have survived the time of great distress; they have washed their robes and made them white in the blood of the Lamb. "For this reason they stand before God's throne/ and worship him day and night in his temple./ The one who sits on the throne will shelter them./ They will not hunger or thirst anymore,/ nor will the sun or any heat strike them./ For the Lamb who is in the center of the throne/ will shepherd them/ and lead them to springs of life-giving water,/ and God will wipe away every tear from their eyes."

GOSPEL
- John 10:27-30 -

Jesus said: "My sheep hear my voice; I know them, and they follow me. I give them eternal life, and they shall never perish. No one can take them out of my hand. My Father, who has given them to me, is greater than all, and no one can take them out of the Father's hand. The Father and I are one."

Sunday

OPENING PRAYER

The Lord is my shepherd;
there is nothing I lack.
In green pastures he makes me lie down;
to still waters he leads me;
he restores my soul.
He guides me along right paths
for the sake of his name.
Even though I walk through the valley of the
shadow of death,
I will fear no evil, for you are with me;
Your rod and your staff comfort me.

You set a table before me
In front of my enemies;
You anoint my head with oil;
my cup overflows.
Indeed, goodness and mercy will pursue me
all the days of my life;
I will dwell in the house of the Lord
for endless days.—Psalm 23 (NABRE)

Good and gracious God, we come humbly before you asking for your guidance and grace. In times when we encounter difficulty or trial, allow us to respond with trust and faithfulness. In times when you ask us to follow your example, let us give our entire selves as you did. In times of disunity or division, give us the strength to unite ever more with the Body of Christ. We thank you for the gift of the Body of Christ. We ask that you help us to remain united as one flock under one shepherd. Amen.

—Prayer for Christian Unity in Times of Peril

LECTIO DIVINA ❧ SACRED READING OF SCRIPTURE

Feel free to take notes on the video reflection in the space below.

LECTIO DIVINA ❧ MEDITATION

This week's Gospel is all about "who are the real followers of Jesus?" Who are the Christians? Who are the shepherds of the flock today?

The Gospel reading indicates that the sheep follow in the example of their shepherd, Jesus. Elsewhere in the Gospels, specifically in John 10:11, Jesus says, "I am the good shepherd. The good shepherd lays down his life for the sheep." How can we lay down our lives for our fellow Christians each day?

How will these sacrifices help us to grow in Christian unity?

LECTIO DIVINA 🕊 PRAYER & RESOLUTION

PRAYER: Let us begin our time of prayer by placing ourselves in this scene in Jerusalem with Jesus teaching his disciples about following him as the good shepherd. Imagine that Jesus has just said that no one can take his flock out of his hand. How does his willingness to lay down his life for his sheep make him a trustworthy shepherd who will never lose his sheep? Just as Jesus laid down his life for his flock, you now recognize this call extends to you as well. Ask Jesus to show you how you can lay down your life for others, seeking to deepen Christian unity.

RESOLUTION: With the guidance of the Holy Spirit, choose one or two ways you can sacrificially give of yourself for others this week to deepen the unity of Christ's flock, whether that be in your family, your workplace, your parish, or another community setting. When you do so, offer up your sacrifices (and possibly sufferings) for the unity of all Christians.

"Greater love no man has than this; that he lay down his life for his friends."
—John 15:13 (RSV)

Monday

Reread the first reading from the Acts of the Apostles (Acts 13:14; 43-52). In it, St. Paul proclaims that the Jews were called to be a "light" to the Gentiles. Reflect on how you can be a light of faith to others in your life, particularly those who do not know the merciful love of Jesus.

> "Darkness cannot put out the light. It can only make God brighter."
>
> —Anonymous

Tuesday

Recall in the Gospel reading when Jesus said, "My sheep hear my voice" (John 10:27). Do you try to hear the voice of Christ in your daily life? How can you be more open to his voice?

> "It's not that the Christian faith has been tried and found wanting, but rather it's been found difficult and left untried."—G.K. Chesterton

Wednesday

Reread the second reading from the Book of Revelation (Revelation 7:9, 14b-17). In this reading, St. John is given a vision of the early Christian martyrs being rewarded in heaven for their service to the kingdom of God. Ask Jesus to give you the heart of a martyr, willing to suffer for the kingdom.

"The believing have, in love, the character of God the Father by Jesus Christ by whom, if we are not in readiness to die into his suffering, his life is not in us."—St. Ignatius of Antioch

Thursday

In the first reading from the Acts of the Apostles, concentrate on the word "joy" from the final verse (Acts 13:52). Ask Jesus to give you a spirit of joy this week, even through the difficult moments.

"All joy emphasizes our pilgrim status; always reminds, beckons, awakens desire. Our best havings are wantings." —C.S. Lewis

Friday

As you read the Gospel passage for this week (John 10:27-30), notice how Jesus reassures his disciples that nothing can separate the faithful from their God. When do you experience closeness with God?

"Prayer is the exercise of drawing on the grace of God."
—Oswald Chambers

Saturday

As you look over this week's readings one more time, reflect on one word or phrase that has continually stood out. What is Jesus trying to reveal to you through this phrase?

"Pray as though everything depended on God. Work as though everything depended on you." —St. Ignatius Loyola

5TH SUNDAY OF EASTER
~ YEAR C ~

EMBRACING THE CROSS

READINGS FOR THE FIFTH SUNDAY OF EASTER

FIRST READING
- Acts 13:14, 43-52 -

After Paul and Barnabas had proclaimed the good news to that city and made a considerable number of disciples, they returned to Lystra and to Iconium and to Antioch. They strengthened the spirits of the disciples and exhorted them to persevere in the faith, saying, "It is necessary for us to undergo many hardships to enter the kingdom of God." They appointed elders for them in each church and, with prayer and fasting, commended them to the Lord in whom they had put their faith. Then they traveled through Pisidia and reached Pamphylia. After proclaiming the word at Perga they went down to Attalia. From there they sailed to Antioch, where they had been commended to the grace of God for the work they had now accomplished. And when they arrived, they called the church together and reported what God had done with them and how he had opened the door of faith to the Gentiles.

RESPONSORIAL PSALM
- Psalm 145:8-9, 10-11, 12-13 -

R: **I will praise your name forever, my king and my God.**
or R: **Alleluia**

The LORD is gracious and merciful,
slow to anger and of great kindness.
The LORD is good to all
and compassionate toward all his works.
R:

Let all your works give you thanks, O LORD,
and let your faithful ones bless you.
Let them discourse of the glory of your kingdom
and speak of your might.
R:

Let them make known your might to the children of Adam,
and the glorious splendor of your kingdom.
Your kingdom is a kingdom for all ages,
and your dominion endures through all generations.
R:

SECOND READING

- Revelation 21:1-5a -

Then I, John, saw a new heaven and a new earth. The former heaven and the former earth had passed away, and the sea was no more. I also saw the holy city, a new Jerusalem, coming down out of heaven from God, prepared as a bride adorned for her husband. I heard a loud voice from the throne saying, "Behold, God's dwelling is with the human race. He will dwell with them and they will be his people and God himself will always be with them as their God. He will wipe every tear from their eyes, and there shall be no more death or mourning, wailing or pain, for the old order has passed away."

The One who sat on the throne said, "Behold, I make all things new."

GOSPEL

- John 13:31-33a, 34-35 -

When Judas had left them, Jesus said, "Now is the Son of Man glorified, and God is glorified in him. If God is glorified in him, God will also glorify him in himself, and God will glorify him at once. My children, I will be with you only a little while longer. I give you a new commandment: love one another. As I have loved you, so you also should love one another. This is how all will know that you are my disciples, if you have love for one another."

Sunday

OPENING PRAYER

Behold me, my beloved Jesus,
weighed down under the burden of my trials and sufferings,
I cast myself at your feet,
that you may renew my strength and my courage,
while I rest here in your Presence.
Permit me to lay down my cross in your Sacred Heart,
for only your infinite goodness can sustain me;
only your love can help me bear my cross;
only your powerful hand can lighten its weight.
O Divine King, Jesus,
whose heart is so compassionate to the afflicted,
I wish to live in you;
suffer and die in you.
During my life be to me my model and my support;
At the hour of my death,
be my hope and my refuge. Amen.

(From http://www.catholic.org/prayers/prayer.php?p=873)

LECTIO DIVINA ✤ SACRED READING OF SCRIPTURE

Feel free to take notes on the video reflection in the space below.

LECTIO DIVINA ✤ MEDITATION

In the video, the presenter uses the term "dandelion theology" to express a mystery of the spiritual life. What is the purpose of the dandelion story he tells?

What character in the image did you first identify with? Was it the little boy? Was it a surprise to turn the image around and picture yourself as the mother?

In the Gospel reading for today, Jesus knows Judas is going to betray him and he will suffer and die very soon, and yet he says, "Now is the Son of Man glorified." He knows that it is only through acceptance of his suffering that he will come into his fullness at the right hand of the Father. How is this a lesson for us when we face trials and suffering?

As we think about the lessons of today's Gospel reading, what are some of the areas in your life where you are not being receptive to the cross?

Is there some trial or inconvenience in your life that you keep avoiding? Or some difficulty or suffering that you keep trying to steer clear of?

LECTIO DIVINA ✦ PRAYER & RESOLUTION

PRAYER: Take a few minutes to consider the words of Jesus: "Now is the Son of Man glorified, and God is glorified in him." Then think about when he said this to the apostles—in the Upper Room, just prior to his death, but also just prior to his Resurrection. Now think about a situation that is causing you pain and suffering. Allow yourself to feel all the emotions surrounding that situation—fear, pressure, pain, sorrow. Now imagine that Jesus is standing before you. He knows all about your situation and he says to you, "Now are you glorified and now God is glorified in you." What do think when you hear Jesus' words? How does hearing that God is glorified through your pain help you look at your situation differently? How can you see your suffering in a new way, knowing that God can bring some good from it?

RESOLUTION: As you are praying, be receptive to the prompting of the Holy Spirit. Ask God to show you ways in which you have been resisting your suffering. Then ask to be shown how you can practice greater receptivity to the cross in your life this week. As God reveals an area for you to focus on, remember that this is his initiative. He will provide grace, and you can cooperate with his grace to experience change.

"If God sends you many sufferings, it is a sign that he has great plans for you and certainly wants to make you a saint."—St. Ignatius of Loyola

Monday

Mary is a powerful figure in our Catholic faith who shows a deep capacity for embracing suffering and difficulty. How is Mary a great model for us in the spiritual life, particularly in regards to embracing the cross? Invite Mary to journey with you this week, and ask her to pray for greater and greater receptivity to the crosses in your life.

> *"In the Eucharist the Church is as it were at the foot of the cross with Mary, united with the offering and intercession of Christ."*
>
> —CCC 1370

Tuesday

Reread the first reading, Acts 14:21-27. What does St. Paul say about hardship? In light of the theme of "Embracing the Cross" this week, how does this speak to you?

"Love and sacrifice are closely linked, like the sun and the light. We cannot love without suffering and we cannot suffer without love."—St. Gianna Molla

Wednesday

Reread Revelation 21:5 from the second reading. As you spend this week uniquely focused on the "poverty" in your life, a good point for us to acknowledge is that Jesus makes all things new. How have you already experienced this reality in your life? How has Jesus made even the hardships and struggles of your life "new"?

"See, I am doing something new!/ Now it springs forth, do you not perceive it?/ In the desert I make a way,/ in the wasteland, rivers."
—Isaiah 43:19

Thursday

Looking at the Gospel reading again, John 13:31-33a, 34-35, what is the new commandment Jesus gives his disciples? How does the Lord want this to be applied in your life this week?

"'A new commandment I give to you, that you love one another, even as I have loved you, that you also love one another. By this all men will know that you are my disciples, if you have love for one another' (John 13:34-35). With these words of Jesus the Gospel of today's Mass ends. In this saying we find the summing up of all holiness." —Blessed Pope John Paul II

Friday

Reread last Sunday's responsorial psalm, Psalm 145:8-13. How is God speaking into your heart through this exhortation? How is it related to the theme of embracing the cross this week?

"Dear brothers and sisters, I pray God may open your eyes and let you see what hidden treasures he bestows on us in the trials from which the world thinks only to flee. Shame turns into honor when we seek God's glory. Present afflictions become the source of heavenly glory. To those who suffer wounds in fighting his battles God opens his arms in loving, tender friendship."

—Oswald Chambers

Saturday

As this week's reflections come to an end, take time to consider again how the Lord is inviting you to embrace the sufferings and hardships of your daily life, even the small things. Read the second reading again, Revelation 21:1-5a. Focus particularly on verses 3-5. How is God encouraging you through these words?

"In this new universe, the heavenly Jerusalem, God will have his dwelling among men. 'He will wipe away every tear from their eyes, and death shall be no more, neither shall there be mourning nor crying nor pain any more, for the former things have passed away.'" —CCC 1044

6TH SUNDAY OF EASTER
～ YEAR C ～

THE HOLY SPIRIT IN THE LIFE OF THE CHURCH

READINGS FOR THE SIXTH SUNDAY OF EASTER

FIRST READING
- Acts 15:1-2, 22-29 -

Some who had come down from Judea were instructing the brothers, "Unless you are circumcised according to the Mosaic practice, you cannot be saved." Because there arose no little dissension and debate by Paul and Barnabas with them, it was decided that Paul, Barnabas, and some of the others should go up to Jerusalem to the apostles and elders about this question.

The apostles and elders, in agreement with the whole church, decided to choose representatives and to send them to Antioch with Paul and Barnabas. The ones chosen were Judas, who was called Barsabbas, and Silas, leaders among the brothers. This is the letter delivered by them:

"The apostles and the elders, your brothers, to the brothers in Antioch, Syria, and Cilicia of Gentile origin: greetings. Since we have heard that some of our number who went out without any mandate from us have upset you with their teachings and disturbed your peace of mind, we have with one accord decided to choose representatives and to send them to you along with our beloved Barnabas and Paul, who have dedicated their lives to the name of our Lord Jesus Christ. So we are sending Judas and Silas who will also convey this same message by word of mouth: 'It is the decision of the Holy Spirit and of us not to place on you any burden beyond these necessities, namely, to abstain from meat sacrificed to idols, from blood, from meats of strangled animals, and from unlawful marriage. If you keep free of these, you will be doing what is right. Farewell.'"

RESPONSORIAL PSALM
-Psalm 67:2-3, 5, 6, 8 -

R: **O God, let all the nations praise you!**
or R: **Alleluia**

May God have pity on us and bless us;
may he let his face shine upon us.
So may your way be known upon earth;
among all nations, your salvation.
R:

May the nations be glad and exult
because you rule the peoples in equity;
the nations on the earth you guide.
R:

May the peoples praise you, O God;
may all the peoples praise you!
May God bless us,
and may all the ends of the earth fear him!
R:

SECOND READING
- Revelation 21:10-14, 22-23 -

*The angel took me in spirit to a great, high mountain and showed
me the holy city Jerusalem coming down out of heaven from God.
It gleamed with the splendor of God. Its radiance was like that of
a precious stone, like jasper, clear as crystal. It had a massive, high
wall, with twelve gates where twelve angels were stationed and
on which names were inscribed, the names of the twelve tribes of
the Israelites. There were three gates facing east, three north, three
south, and three west. The wall of the city had twelve courses of
stones as its foundation, on which were inscribed the twelve names
of the twelve apostles of the Lamb.*

*I saw no temple in the city for its temple is the Lord God almighty
and the Lamb. The city had no need of sun or moon to shine on it,
for the glory of God gave it light, and its lamp was the Lamb.*

GOSPEL

- John 14:23-29 -

Jesus said to his disciples: "Whoever loves me will keep my word, and my Father will love him, and we will come to him and make our dwelling with him. Whoever does not love me does not keep my words; yet the word you hear is not mine but that of the Father who sent me.

"I have told you this while I am with you. The Advocate, the Holy Spirit, whom the Father will send in my name, will teach you everything and remind you of all that I told you. Peace I leave with you; my peace I give to you. Not as the world gives do I give it to you. Do not let your hearts be troubled or afraid. You heard me tell you, 'I am going away and I will come back to you.' If you loved me, you would rejoice that I am going to the Father; for the Father is greater than I. And now I have told you this before it happens, so that when it happens you may believe."

Sunday

OPENING PRAYER

Come, Holy Spirit, fill the hearts of your faithful and kindle in them the fire of your love. Send forth your Spirit and they shall be created. And you shall renew the face of the earth.

O God, who by the light of the Holy Spirit, did instruct the hearts of the faithful, grant that by the same Holy Spirit we may be truly wise and ever enjoy his consolations. Through Christ our Lord. Amen.

LECTIO DIVINA ✒ SACRED READING OF SCRIPTURE

Feel free to take notes on the video reflection in the space below.

LECTIO DIVINA ✒ MEDITATION

This week's first reading from the Acts of the Apostles shows us not simply the humanity of the apostles but also the divine guidance they received from the Holy Spirit. How did the early church deal with difficult questions, and what does this mean for us today?

According to the Gospel reading, what is the role of the Holy Spirit in the lives of the apostles?

Why might it be difficult for some Catholics today to believe the Holy Spirit continues to guide the teaching of the Church?

LECTIO DIVINA ✒ PRAYER & RESOLUTION

PRAYER: Imagine that you are in the presence of Jesus. He says to you the words he spoke in today's Gospel reading, "Peace I leave with you; my peace I give to you. Not as the world gives do I give it to you. Do not let your hearts be troubled or afraid." As you hear his words, ask yourself if there is something troubling you or creating fear. If so, ask Jesus how you can overcome your anxiety. Now calmly pray the following words: "Come, Holy Spirit." Trust and believe that the Holy Spirit is with you, bringing you the peace Jesus promised.

RESOLUTION: This week, whenever you feel anxious or worried, remember that Jesus promised that the Holy Spirit would be with us through the Church until the end of time. What is one practical thing you can do to remind yourself of that reality?

"Just as in one man there is one soul and one body, yet many members; even so the Catholic Church is one body, having many members. The soul that quickens this body is the Holy Spirit; and therefore in the Creed after confessing our belief in the Holy Spirit, we are bid to believe in the Holy Catholic Church."—St. Elizabeth Ann Seton

Monday

The first reading, Acts 15:1-2, 22-29, gives us a glimpse into the life of the earliest Christians. Take some time and reflect on your journey as a Christian, from your Baptism until the present.

"I will go peaceably and firmly to the Catholic Church: for if faith is so important to our salvation, I will seek it where true faith first began, seek it among those who received it from God himself."

—St. Elizabeth Ann Seton

Tuesday

Reflect today on how the Holy Spirit speaks through Scripture and the teaching of the Church. Is there some area of church teaching that you feel you should investigate further in order to be able to explain and defend it?

"Comfort in tribulation can be secured only on the sure ground of faith holding as true the words of Scripture and the teaching of the Catholic Church."—St. Thomas More

275

Wednesday

Prayerfully and slowly reread the second reading from the Book of Revelation (Revelation 21:10-14, 22-23), and allow yourself to visualize the heavenly city that John is describing. Place yourself in that city and reflect on the immense joy you are experiencing.

"The Church, a communion living in the faith of the apostles which she transmits, is the place where we know the Holy Spirit."

—CCC 688

Thursday

The responsorial psalm for this week prays that all nations will know and praise the Lord. Take some time now to pray for the conversion of our world, that indeed one day all will be reunited in the Lamb.

"Truly, matters in the world are in a bad state; but if you and I begin in earnest to reform ourselves, a really good beginning will have been made."—St. Peter of Alcantara

Friday

Reread the Gospel passage for this week (John 14:23-29), and entrust everything you have to the Holy Spirit. Ask the Holy Spirit for the grace to trust God in all things.

> *"Leave sadness to those in the world. We who work for God should be lighthearted."*
>
> —St. Leonard of Port Maurice

Saturday

As you look over this week's readings, take some time to thank Jesus for the gift of faith. Think about how you can better express your faith through a more regular participation in the sacraments.

"The Cross is the way to Paradise, but only when it is borne willingly."

—St. Paul of the Cross

THE ASCENSION
OF THE LORD
❧ YEAR C ❧

I WILL BE WITH YOU ALWAYS

READINGS FOR THE ASCENSION OF THE LORD

FIRST READING
- Acts 1:1-11 -

In the first book, Theophilus, I dealt with all that Jesus did and taught until the day he was taken up, after giving instructions through the Holy Spirit to the apostles whom he had chosen. He presented himself alive to them by many proofs after he had suffered, appearing to them during forty days and speaking about the kingdom of God. While meeting with them, he enjoined them not to depart from Jerusalem, but to wait for "the promise of the Father about which you have heard me speak; for John baptized with water, but in a few days you will be baptized with the Holy Spirit."

When they had gathered together they asked him, "Lord, are you at this time going to restore the kingdom to Israel?" He answered them, "It is not for you to know the times or seasons that the Father has established by his own authority. But you will receive power when the Holy Spirit comes upon you, and you will be my witnesses in Jerusalem, throughout Judea and Samaria, and to the ends of the earth." When he had said this, as they were looking on, he was lifted up, and a cloud took him from their sight. While they were looking intently at the sky as he was going, suddenly two men dressed in white garments stood beside them. They said, "Men of Galilee, why are you standing there looking at the sky? This Jesus who has been taken up from you into heaven will return in the same way as you have seen him going into heaven.

RESPONSORIAL PSALM

- Psalm 47:2-3, 6-7, 8-9 -

R: **God mounts his throne to shouts of joy:**
a blare of trumpets for the Lord.

or R: **Alleluia**

All you peoples, clap your hands,
shout to God with cries of gladness,
for the LORD, the Most High, the awesome,
is the great king over all the earth.
R:

God mounts his throne amid shouts of joy;
the LORD, amid trumpet blasts.
Sing praise to God, sing praise;
sing praise to our king, sing praise.
R:

For king of all the earth is God;
sing hymns of praise.
God reigns over the nations,
God sits upon his holy throne.
R:

SECOND READING

- Ephesians 1:17-23 -

*Brothers and sisters: May the God of our Lord Jesus Christ,
the Father of glory, give you a Spirit of wisdom and revelation
resulting in knowledge of him. May the eyes of your hearts be
enlightened, that you may know what is the hope that belongs to his
call, what are the riches of glory in his inheritance among the holy
ones, and what is the surpassing greatness of his power for us who
believe, in accord with the exercise of his great might: which he
worked in Christ, raising him from the dead and seating him at his
right hand in the heavens, far above every principality, authority,
power, and dominion, and every name that is named not only in
this age but also in the one to come. And he put all things beneath
his feet and gave him as head over all things to the church, which is
his body, the fullness of the one who fills all things in every way.*

OPTIONAL SECOND READING
- Hebrews 9:24-28; 10:19-23 -

Christ did not enter into a sanctuary made by hands, a copy of the true one, but heaven itself, that he might now appear before God on our behalf. Not that he might offer himself repeatedly, as the high priest enters each year into the sanctuary with blood that is not his own; if that were so, he would have had to suffer repeatedly from the foundation of the world. But now once for all he has appeared at the end of the ages to take away sin by his sacrifice. Just as it is appointed that men and women die once, and after this the judgment, so also Christ, offered once to take away the sins of many, will appear a second time, not to take away sin but to bring salvation to those who eagerly await him.

Therefore, brothers and sisters, since through the blood of Jesus we have confidence of entrance into the sanctuary by the new and living way he opened for us through the veil, that is, his flesh, and since we have "a great priest over the house of God," let us approach with a sincere heart and in absolute trust, with our hearts sprinkled clean from an evil conscience and our bodies washed in pure water. Let us hold unwaveringly to our confession that gives us hope, for he who made the promise is trustworthy.

GOSPEL
- Luke 24:46-53 -

Jesus said to his disciples: "Thus it is written that the Christ would suffer and rise from the dead on the third day and that repentance, for the forgiveness of sins, would be preached in his name to all the nations, beginning from Jerusalem. You are witnesses of these things. And behold I am sending the promise of my Father upon you; but stay in the city until you are clothed with power from on high."

Then he led them out as far as Bethany, raised his hands, and blessed them. As he blessed them he parted from them and was taken up to heaven. They did him homage and then returned to Jerusalem with great joy, and they were continually in the temple praising God.

Sunday

OPENING PRAYER

O King of Glory,
Who didst this day ascend in triumph
above all the heavens!
Leave us not orphans,
but send upon us the Spirit of Truth,
promised by the Father. Alleluia!

LECTIO DIVINA ❧ SACRED READING OF SCRIPTURE

Feel free to take notes on the video reflection in the space below.

LECTIO DIVINA ❧ MEDITATION

According to the presenter, what does it mean that Jesus ascended into heaven?

How is Jesus' Ascension a message of good news for the disciples and Christ's followers today?

Take time to consider the question the presenter asked at the end of the video: Am I aware that through the sacraments I am clothed with power from on high—in other words, with the Holy Spirit?

LECTIO DIVINA ❧ PRAYER & RESOLUTION

PRAYER: Place yourself in the position of one of Christ's followers. You've been with Jesus for forty days. Now he tells you it's time for him to leave. You go out into the countryside and watch as he rises into the sky, and soon disappears. What sorts of emotions are you experiencing? Are you afraid? sad? Now recall that just before he left, he promised never to abandon you, and he assured you that help would soon come in the form of the Holy Spirit. Now how do you feel? What would you say to the people around you? As you walk back to the town, what might you talk about?

RESOLUTION: Just as the disciples were given a great mission to spread Christ's kingdom to the ends of the earth, so too does each of us carry a unique mission through the power of the Holy Spirit. This week ask God to show you what this mission is in your life, and choose one small way that you can carry out your mission as a follower of Christ.

"Our Lord prefers to wait himself for the sinner for years rather than keep him waiting one instant."—St. Peter Julian Eymard

Monday

How does the Ascension leave us with a message of hope? How can you better live out Christian hope in your life?

> "Hope is practiced through the virtue of patience, which continues to do good even in the face of apparent failure, and through the virtue of humility, which accepts God's mystery and trusts him even at times of darkness."
>
> —Pope Benedict XVI

Tuesday

Jesus remained with his disciples for forty days before he ascended into heaven, "speaking about the kingdom of God" (Acts 1:3). Imagine you are with Jesus during those forty days; what kinds of things does Jesus tell you? Reflect on what messages you think would have been necessary for the disciples after having just witnessed the Resurrection.

> "If one does away with the fact of the Resurrection, one also does away with the Cross, for both stand and fall together, and one would then have to find a new center for the whole message of the gospel." —Hans Urs von Balthasar

Wednesday

Reread the passage from St. Paul's letter in the second reading (Ephesians 1:17-23). Take some time to reflect on the magnitude of hope that we receive through Christ's paschal mystery, and thank God for the gift of that hope in your own life.

"Go forth in peace, for you have followed the good road. Go forth without fear, for he who created you has made you holy, has always protected you, and loves you as a mother. Blessed be you, my God, for having created me."

—St. Clare of Assisi

Thursday

The responsorial psalm for this week calls us to "sing praise" to God in heaven (Psalm 47:6-7). How do you praise God in your daily life? Do you frequently and regularly make the time to show God honor and praise?

"In the inexpressible joy of this eternal vision, human nature will possess what eye has not seen or ear heard, what man's heart has never conceived."—Pope St. Leo the Great

Friday

Last Sunday's first reading (Acts 1:1-11) promises that Jesus will one day return. What are you doing to prepare for his return? Reflect on how you can prepare your heart for the return of your king.

> "Christ's Ascension into heaven signifies his participation, in his humanity, in God's power and authority. Jesus Christ is Lord: He possesses all power in heaven and on earth."
>
> —CCC 668

Saturday

As you look over last Sunday's readings one more time, reflect on the gift of the Ascension of Jesus. When you do so, pick out one word or phrase that has continually stood out in your prayer life this week. Why do you think God has chosen to reveal this to you?

"I pray because I can't help myself. I pray because I'm helpless. I pray because the need flows out of me all the time, waking and sleeping. It doesn't change God, it changes me."—C.S. Lewis

7TH SUNDAY
OF EASTER
ᕷ YEAR C ᕷ

AND I
IN THEM

READINGS FOR THE SEVENTH SUNDAY OF EASTER

FIRST READING
- Acts 7:55-60 -

Stephen, filled with the Holy Spirit, looked intently to heaven and saw the glory of God and Jesus standing at the right hand of God, and said, "Behold, I see the heavens opened and the Son of Man standing at the right side of God." But they cried out in a loud voice, covered their ears, and rushed upon him together. They threw him out of the city, and began to stone him. The witnesses laid down their cloaks at the feet of a young man named Saul. As they were stoning Stephen, he called out, "Lord Jesus, receive my spirit." Then he fell to his knees and cried out in a loud voice, "Lord, do not hold this sin against them"; and when he said this, he fell asleep.

RESPONSORIAL PSALM
- Psalm 97:1-2, 6-7, 9 -

R: **The Lord is king, the most high over all the earth**
or R: **Alleluia**

The LORD is king; let the earth rejoice;
let the many islands be glad.
Justice and judgment are the foundation of his throne.
R:

The heavens proclaim his justice,
and all peoples see his glory.
All gods are prostrate before him.
R:

You, O LORD, are the Most High over all the earth,
exalted far above all gods.
R:

SECOND READING
- Revelation 22:12-14, 16-17, 20 -

I, John, heard a voice saying to me: "Behold, I am coming soon. I bring with me the recompense I will give to each according to his deeds. I am the Alpha and the Omega, the first and the last, the beginning and the end."

Blessed are they who wash their robes so as to have the right to the tree of life and enter the city through its gates.

"I, Jesus, sent my angel to give you this testimony for the churches. I am the root and offspring of David, the bright morning star."

The Spirit and the bride say, "Come." Let the hearer say, "Come." Let the one who thirsts come forward, and the one who wants it receive the gift of life-giving water.

The one who gives this testimony says, "Yes, I am coming soon." Amen! Come, Lord Jesus!

GOSPEL
- John 17:20-26 -

Lifting up his eyes to heaven, Jesus prayed saying: "Holy Father, I pray not only for them, but also for those who will believe in me through their word, so that they may all be one, as you, Father, are in me and I in you, that they also may be in us, that the world may believe that you sent me. And I have given them the glory you gave me, so that they may be one, as we are one, I in them and you in me, that they may be brought to perfection as one, that the world may know that you sent me, and that you loved them even as you loved me. Father, they are your gift to me. I wish that where I am they also may be with me, that they may see my glory that you gave me, because you loved me before the foundation of the world. Righteous Father, the world also does not know you, but I know you, and they know that you sent me. I made known to them your name and I will make it known, that the love with which you loved me may be in them and I in them."

Sunday

OPENING PRAYER

Almighty God,
Through Jesus you say to us
that whoever wishes to be first must become the
least and the servant of all.
We enter into your presence,
knowing that your victory is won through the
powerlessness of the cross.
We come to pray that your church may be one.
Teach us to accept humbly that this unity is a
gift of your Spirit;
Through this gift, change and transform us
and make us more like your Son Jesus Christ.
Amen.

—Opening Prayer from the Ecumenical Worship Service

LECTIO DIVINA 🕊 SACRED READING OF SCRIPTURE

Feel free to take notes on the video reflection in the space below.

LECTIO DIVINA 🕊 MEDITATION

The central plea of Jesus' "priestly prayer," which he offered the night before he died, was for the unity of his followers. According to the presenter in the video, how are Christians united with Christ?

Even though Christ calls his followers to imitate the union of the most holy Trinity, history would remind us that this is much easier said than done. How does Christ assist us in achieving unity with other Christians?

What did Christ say in today's Gospel reading that gives us clues to this assistance?

LECTIO DIVINA 🕊 PRAYER & RESOLUTION

PRAYER: Place yourself in today's Gospel reading, and imagine being in the room with Jesus and his disciples at the Last Supper. Jesus sits up and begins to talk. Listen attentively to his prayer to the Heavenly Father. In the last moments of his life—his darkest time—he's thinking of and praying for you. Hear his words now and fill in your own name at the pause: "I pray not only for these, but also for (_____), so that they may all be one, as you, Father, are in me and I in you, that (_____) also may be in us, that the world may believe that you sent me….Father, (_____) is your gift to me." Now open your heart to his words, and ask Jesus what part you can play in making "all be one."

RESOLUTION: Prayerfully consider how you can be more of a source of unity in your family, parish, workplace, or community. It may be helpful to think of one person with whom you frequently experience discord, disagreement, or tension. Spend this week offering up your prayers for that person, and find some time to reach out to that person in Christian love.

"In necessary things, unity;
in doubtful things, liberty;
in all things, charity."
—St. Augustine

Monday

Reread the first reading (Acts 7:55-60). Reflect on the courage and witness of the first martyr of the Church, St. Stephen. Ask Jesus to give you that same spirit of courage and conviction for the faith.

"The principal act of courage is to endure and withstand dangers doggedly rather than to attack them."

—St. Thomas Aquinas

Tuesday

In the first reading from the Acts of the Apostles, we see Stephen praying for his persecutors in the final moments of his life (Acts 7:60). Take this time to pray for those who may persecute you or those whom you simply struggle to get along with. Use the example of St. Stephen to always pray for your enemies and persecutors.

"First let a little love find entrance in their hearts, and the rest will follow."—St. Philip Neri

Wednesday

Reread the second reading, Revelation 22:12-14, 16-17, 20. As you read, focus on the phrase "I am the Alpha and the Omega, the first and the last, the beginning and the end." Reflect on the power and beauty of God who has been and always will be present.

"God, infinitely perfect and blessed in himself, in a plan of sheer goodness freely created man to make him share in his own blessed life. For this reason, at every time and in every place, God draws close to man."
—CCC 1

Thursday

The second reading from the Book of Revelation speaks of thirsting for the life-giving waters of God (Revelation 22:17). As Christians, we know we receive this life-giving water through the gift of our Baptism. Spend some time reflecting on the gift of Baptism and the baptismal promises you confess each week at Mass.

"The Lord was baptized, not to be cleansed himself, but to cleanse the waters, so that those waters, cleansed by the flesh of Christ which knew no sin, might have the power of Baptism."—St. Ambrose of Milan

Friday

As you reread this week's Gospel reading, John 17:20-26, pray for the gift of unity in your own life. Is there anyone in your life you feel disconnected from or are estranged from? Pray for that relationship and for a charitable reconciliation.

> *"Mount Calvary is the academy of love."*
> —St. Francis de Sales

Saturday

As you look over this week's Gospel reading one more time, reflect on the theme of this past week "and I in them" (John 17:26). How have you seen God acting in your life this week?

> *"The Church is a virgin, the bride of one spouse, who is Christ, and this Church does not allow herself to be violated by any error; so that, throughout the whole world there may be for us one uncorruptedness of a single chaste communion."* —St. Leo the Great

PENTECOST SUNDAY

❧ YEAR C ❧

CHANGED, TRANSFORMED, RENEWED

READINGS FOR PENTECOST SUNDAY

FIRST READING
- Acts 2:1–11 -

When the time for Pentecost was fulfilled, they were all in one place together. And suddenly there came from the sky a noise like a strong driving wind, and it filled the entire house in which they were. Then there appeared to them tongues as of fire, which parted and came to rest on each one of them. And they were all filled with the Holy Spirit and began to speak in different tongues, as the Spirit enabled them to proclaim.

Now there were devout Jews from every nation under heaven staying in Jerusalem. At this sound, they gathered in a large crowd, but they were confused because each one heard them speaking in his own language. They were astounded, and in amazement they asked, "Are not all these people who are speaking Galileans? Then how does each of us hear them in his native language? We are Parthians, Medes, and Elamites, inhabitants of Mesopotamia, Judea and Cappadocia, Pontus and Asia, Phrygia and Pamphylia, Egypt and the districts of Libya near Cyrene, as well as travelers from Rome, both Jews and converts to Judaism, Cretans and Arabs, yet we hear them speaking in our own tongues of the mighty acts of God."

RESPONSORIAL PSALM
- Psalm 104:1, 24, 29-30, 31, 34 -

R: **Lord, send out your Spirit, and renew the face of the earth.**
or R: **Alleluia**

Bless the LORD, O my soul!
O LORD, my God, you are great indeed!
How manifold are your works, O LORD!
The earth is full of your creatures;
R:

May the glory of the LORD endure forever;
may the LORD be glad in his works!
Pleasing to him be my theme;
I will be glad in the LORD.
R:

If you take away their breath, they perish
and return to their dust.
When you send forth your spirit, they are created,
and you renew the face of the earth.
R:

SECOND READING
- 1 Corinthians 12:3b-7, 12-13 -

Brothers and sisters: No one can say, "Jesus is Lord," except by the Holy Spirit.

There are different kinds of spiritual gifts but the same Spirit; there are different forms of service but the same Lord; there are different workings but the same God who produces all of them in everyone. To each individual the manifestation of the Spirit is given for some benefit.

As a body is one though it has many parts, and all the parts of the body, though many, are one body, so also Christ. For in one Spirit we were all baptized into one body, whether Jews or Greeks, slaves or free persons, and we were all given to drink of one Spirit.

OPTIONAL SECOND READING
- Romans 8:8-17 -

Brothers and sisters: Those who are in the flesh cannot please God. But you are not in the flesh; on the contrary, you are in the spirit, if only the Spirit of God dwells in you. Whoever does not have the Spirit of Christ does not belong to him. But if Christ is in you, although the body is dead because of sin, the spirit is alive because of righteousness. If the Spirit of the one who raised Jesus from the dead dwells in you, the one who raised Christ from the dead will give life to your mortal bodies also, through his Spirit that dwells in you. Consequently, brothers and sisters, we are not debtors to the flesh, to live according to the flesh. For if you live according to the flesh, you will die, but if by the Spirit you put to death the deeds of the body, you will live.

For those who are led by the Spirit of God are sons of God. For you did not receive a spirit of slavery to fall back into fear, but you received a Spirit of adoption, through whom we cry, "Abba, Father!" The Spirit himself bears witness with our spirit that we are children of God, and if children, then heirs, heirs of God and joint heirs with Christ, if only we suffer with him so that we may also be glorified with him.

GOSPEL
- John 20:19-23 -

On the evening of that first day of the week, when the doors were locked, where the disciples were, for fear of the Jews, Jesus came and stood in their midst and said to them, "Peace be with you." When he had said this, he showed them his hands and his side. The disciples rejoiced when they saw the Lord. Jesus said to them again, "Peace be with you. As the Father has sent me, so I send you." And when he had said this, he breathed on them and said to them, "Receive the Holy Spirit. Whose sins you forgive are forgiven them, and whose sins you retain are retained."

OPTIONAL GOSPEL READING
- John 14:15-16, 23b-26 -

Jesus said to his disciples: "If you love me, you will keep my commandments. And I will ask the Father, and he will give you another Advocate to be with you always.

"Whoever loves me will keep my word, and my Father will love him, and we will come to him and make our dwelling with him. Those who do not love me do not keep my words; yet the word you hear is not mine but that of the Father who sent me.

"I have told you this while I am with you. The Advocate, the Holy Spirit whom the Father will send in my name, will teach you everything and remind you of all that I told you."

Sunday

OPENING PRAYER

God our Father, let the Spirit you sent on your Church to begin the teaching of the Gospel continue to work in the world through the hearts of all who believe. We ask this through our Lord Jesus Christ, your Son, who lives and reigns with you and the Holy Spirit, one God, forever and ever. Amen.

LECTIO DIVINA ✼ SACRED READING OF SCRIPTURE

Feel free to take notes on the video reflection in the space below.

LECTIO DIVINA ✼ MEDITATION

In the video, the presenter mentioned three ways the New Testament Pentecost experience parallels the giving of the Law at Mount Sinai on the first Pentecost. What are the parallels?

What is one example given in the video of how the Holy Spirit changes us?

In his wisdom, God has given us the Sacrament of Reconciliation, which restores the life of the Holy Spirit within us. How important a gift is this sacrament to you personally, and how might you thank the Holy Spirit for it?

LECTIO DIVINA ❧ PRAYER & RESOLUTION

PRAYER: Imagine being at that first Pentecost and seeing the Holy Spirit fall upon the apostles. You know the apostles as good men, but you also know that they are filled with weakness, pride, and cowardice. One by one, you see them become emboldened by the Holy Spirit to preach the Gospel without fear and become ideal witnesses to Jesus Christ. You see, for example, Peter, who had denied Jesus three times, now taking the lead in publically proclaiming Christ as Messiah and Lord. He is a changed man! You see the others boldly proclaiming their faith. Now if you knew the Holy Spirit were to come to you next, how might you envision your life being changed? If there is one area of personal weakness in your life that you think the Holy Spirit would want to transform the most, what would that be? Take a few moments in prayer to ask God about this.

RESOLUTION: Talk to God about this one area of weakness and ask him how you can work on it this week. Make a particular resolution that would help you improve in this area of weakness and invite the Holy Spirit to give you his strength, just as he strengthened Peter and the apostles at Pentecost long ago.

"The LORD God … blew into his nostrils the breath of life, and so man became a living being."
—Genesis 2:7

Monday

In the Sunday's first reading from Acts 2:1-11, Luke reports, "They were all filled with the Holy Spirit and began to speak in different tongues, as the Spirit enabled them to proclaim." Note how the Holy Spirit prompts a change in external behavior. Pray for wisdom to understand some of the changes in your behavior that you think the Holy Spirit might want to bring about.

"It is the spirit that gives life, while the flesh is of no avail."

—John 6:63

Tuesday

As you reflect on Sunday's second reading (1 Corinthians 12:3b-7, 12-13), consider how Paul stresses the differences of gifts but the unity of their source. You receive particular gifts to benefit the Body of Christ. Spend some time thanking the Holy Spirit for the gifts he has given you, and consider how God might want you to use those gifts for the benefit of others.

"[The Holy Spirit] is the only gift worthy of God: as God, God gives nothing other than God; he gives himself, and thereby gives everything."—Pope Benedict XVI

Wednesday

As Paul notes in 1 Corinthians 12:13, Baptism incorporates people of many cultures, social levels, and backgrounds into one body. Write a short prayer mentioning some of the cultural, social, ethnic, or other differences in your family, parish, or community, thanking God for the Holy Spirit in each of them.

"Thus says the LORD:/ I will pour out my spirit upon all flesh./ Your sons and daughters shall prophesy,/ your old men shall dream dreams,/ your young men shall see visions;/ even upon the servants and handmaids,/ in those days, I will pour out my spirit."
—Joel 3:1-2

Thursday

Reflecting further on cultural, social, and ethnic differences, consider some ways in which they are of benefit to you personally; for example, how the confident faith of those in material poverty can improve your own faith.

"For Wisdom, the artificer of all, taught me./ For in her is a spirit/ intelligent, holy, unique,/ Manifold, subtle, agile,/ clear, unstained, certain,/ Not baneful, loving the good, keen,/ unhampered, beneficent, kindly,/ Firm, secure, tranquil,/ all-powerful, all-seeing,/ And pervading all spirits."—Wisdom 7:22-24

Friday

In the Gospel reading, John 20:19-23, Jesus breathes on the apostles to communicate the Holy Spirit and then gives them authority to forgive sins. In prayer, ask the Holy Spirit to reveal to you one area where you need to seek forgiveness through the Sacrament of Reconciliation.

> *"The Holy Spirit is truly 'spirit' in the fullest possible sense of the word. In all probability we must make our stumbling way to him anew from the midst of a world profoundly changed."*
>
> —Pope Benedict XVI

Saturday

This week, you've reflected on how the Holy Spirit produces behavioral changes in people, builds a unified body from differences among the parts, and moves us to ask for and grant forgiveness—all related to love of neighbor. Now, in your journal, write a short prayer asking the Holy Spirit to help you love him "more than these" (John 21:15).

"As they prayed, the place where they were gathered shook, and they were all filled with the holy Spirit and continued to speak the word of God with boldness."—Acts 4:31

GLOSSARY

ACT OF CONTRITION: A prayer that expresses sorrow for sin and asks for forgiveness.

ADVENT: The period of preparation before Christmas. It begins with the Sunday nearest to the feast of St. Andrew the Apostle (November 30) and continues for four Sundays. Advent is the first season of the Church Year. The name derives from the Latin word adventus meaning "coming."

APOSTOLIC: Relating to the apostles or their teaching, work, or times; or referring to the Pope.

BEATITUDES: The opening verses of Jesus' Sermon on the Mount (Matthew 5:1-12). Jesus states several blessings or "divine favors" bestowed upon a person possessing certain character qualities such as the meek shall inherit the earth.

BLESSED SACRAMENT: The Body and Blood of Christ, received by Catholics who have undergone their first Holy Communion. The soul of the person receiving the Eucharist should be in a "state of grace," that is, no mortal sin on his or her soul at the time of communion.

BRETHREN: Lay members; a subdivision of a larger religious group.

COMMUNION RITE: The celebration of the Eucharist as a paschal meal, following the Lord's command to partake of his Body and Blood as spiritual nourishment. Communion begins with the Lord's Prayer and after a series of liturgical rites, ends with post-Communion prayer.

CONFIRMATION: The Sacrament of Spiritual Strengthening, which strengthens the supernatural life received in Baptism. Confirmation deepens our capacity to remain spiritually alive and confers the assimilation to the character of Jesus the priest, teacher, and king.

DAVIDIC: In relation or pertaining to David, king of Israel and psalmist, or to his family lineage.

DECADE OF THE ROSARY: A division of the rosary that consists primarily of ten Hail Marys. A chaplet of the rosary consists of five decades.

DOCTRINE: The set of beliefs upheld and taught by the Church.

ECUMENICAL COUNCIL: An assembly of bishops and other ecclesiastical representatives of the worldwide Catholic Church. Roman Catholic Canon Law states that this gathering must be initiated and convened by the Pope.

EPIPHANY: The Christian feast, celebrated on January 6, commemorating the manifestation of the divine nature of Jesus to the Gentiles, as represented by the Magi.

EUCHARIST: Derived from a Greek word meaning "thanksgiving," this is the name for the Blessed Sacrament, in which Jesus is truly present. The Eucharist completes Christian initiation and is the foundation and confirmation of Christian practice and belief (CCC 1322-1419).

HOLY WEEK: The week preceding the celebration of Resurrection Sunday (Easter). The week begins with Palm Sunday and includes Maundy Thursday, Good Friday, and Holy Saturday.

INCARNATION: The union of divinity with humanity in the Divine Person of Jesus Christ.

INTERCESSION: The act of saying a prayer or petition on behalf of another person.

LENT: The forty-day season in the Church Year leading up to Easter. It is a season to prepare for Baptism and to renew baptismal commitments. Traditionally, it is a time of fasting, confession, and acts of mercy to strengthen our faith and devotional life. In preparation for Lent, the Church celebrates Mardi Gras (Fat Tuesday or Shrove Tuesday) the day before Ash Wednesday, which is the day the Lenten season begins. The forty days of Lent are biblically significant for two reasons: The Israelites wandered in the desert for forty years, and Jesus spent forty days in the desert, during which he was tempted by Satan.

LITURGICAL: Relating to or having characteristics of the public worship of the Church. The liturgy refers to a pattern of worship used in service and can include the rites, ceremonies, prayers, and sacraments of the Church. A liturgical year consists of a cycle of seasons for the church that determines when feast days, including celebration of saints, are to be observed and which portions of Scripture are to be read in the liturgical cycle. Distinct liturgical colors also appear in connection with the seasons of the liturgical year.

LITURGY OF THE HOURS: The daily prayers of the Catholic Church that are recited at the specified hours of the day.

MAGISTERIUM: The teaching office or authority of the Church, consisting of the Pope and bishops.

MANNA: The food that was miraculously sent to the Israelites during their forty years in the desert. Manna fell from the sky as small white flakes that covered the ground (Exodus 16).

MITRE: The liturgical headdress of a bishop, consisting of a tall, pointed cleft cap, with two bands hanging down the back.

MOSAIC LAW: The first five books of the Hebrew Scriptures that God gave to the Israelites through Moses. The Mosaic Law begins with the Ten Commandments and contains the ancient laws of the Hebrews, also called the "Law of Moses."

NEW COVENANT: The new relationship God has with humanity that began at the first coming of Jesus and that will be completed at his second coming. In Luke 22:20 Jesus says, "This cup is the new covenant in my blood which will be shed for you." For Christians, the New Covenant replaces the old Mosaic Covenant.

OLD COVENANT: The covenant God made with Moses (the Mosaic Covenant) that established the Old Testament laws and God's relationship with the Jewish people.

PASSION: The events and the physical, spiritual, and mental suffering endured by Jesus in the hours starting with the Agony in the Garden and including his trial and death on the cross (CCC 607, 612, 1708, 1992, 2020).

PENITENTIAL RITE: During Mass, a time of reflection on one's sins and a prayer for God's mercy. A time to focus on our sinfulness and say we're sorry for any wrongdoing, knowing with confidence that God is there with us and ready to forgive.

PENTECOST: A feast of the church that commemorates the descent of the Holy Spirit on the apostles fifty days after the Resurrection of Jesus, on the ancient Jewish festival called the Feast of Weeks or Pentecost.

PONTIFICAL COUNCIL: A group of small to midsize agencies, led by a cardinal or archbishop, that is part of the larger organization called the Roman Curia. The Roman Curia helps the Pope in the governance and oversight of the Catholic Church.

PRESBYTERAL: A council of priests within the diocese required by Church (Canon) Law.

REPENTANCE: To die with Christ; giving up our former way of life in favor of the Way, the Truth, and the Life found in Christ himself. It is literally to "change one's mind," so as to be in a union of mind, heart, and soul with the Person of Jesus.

SACRAMENT OF RECONCILIATION: Also known as Penance and Confession, the sacrament in which the priest (as an agent of God) forgives sins committed after Baptism—when sinners are truly sorry for their actions, confess their wrongdoings, and are willing to make satisfaction for them (CCC 1440-1458).

SANCTIFIED: To be set apart for God; living the Christian life; to be absent or becoming absent from sin.

SECOND COMING OF CHRIST: The reappearance of Jesus as judge for the Last Judgment. Christians should be prepared for this time, but it is unpredictable and unknown, according to Scripture.

SEDER SUPPER: A ceremonial meal that commemorates the Exodus from Egypt and includes the eating of symbolic foods. Generally, the meal is held on the first night of Passover for Jews in Israel and on the first and second nights of Passover for Jews and Orthodox living outside of Israel.

SERAPHIM: The first hierarchy of angels who have no direct contact with mankind; they are the angels of God's Presence.

SYMBOLON: "The Greek word symbolon meant half of a broken object, for example, a seal presented as a token of recognition. The broken parts were placed together to verify the bearer's identity. The symbol of faith, then, is a sign of recognition and communion between believers. Symbolon also means a gathering, collection, or summary. A symbol of faith is a summary of the principal truths of the faith and therefore serves as the first and fundamental point of reference for catechesis." —Catechism of the Catholic Church 188.

TORAH: The first five books of the Hebrew Scriptures; the law of God as revealed to Moses. In Judaism, these books are called the "Torah."

TRANSFIGURATION: The Christian feast, celebrated on August 6, which commemorates the emanation of radiance from the Person of Jesus that occurred on a mountain (CCC 554-556).

TRINITARIAN: An individual who believes in the doctrine of the Trinity—Father, Son, and Holy Spirit.